True Wealth of Nations

A story of how money became dishonest money

True Wealth of Nations

First published 2008.
Second Edition reprinted 2014 by CreateSpace.

ISBN-13: 978-1497456167
ISBN-10: 1497456169

Category: Business & Economics.
Author: Stefan B Sigfried.

Available at www. createspace.com and other places.

true wealth 6by9 v10_7e_createspace, 2014-03-26.

Revolutions are not made; they come. A revolution is as natural a growth as an oak. It comes out of the past. Its foundations are laid far back.

Wendell Phillips

Imagination is more important than knowledge.

Albert Einstein

A book that furnishes no quotations is, me judice, no book—it is a plaything.

Thomas Love Peacock

Contents

Preface

For the love of money is a root of all kinds of evil. [1 Timothy 6:10]

We read about increasing national debt in the US and other places and that this threatens to give us an economic meltdown. It is suggested that a solution is that banks should be nationalized. Explanations are given that it is the way banks can create their own money through the fractional reserve system that is the real problem. In fact some even go so far as to say that if there were no debt there would be no money! The crisis, the economic bubbles and the extremely unfair distribution of wealth are discussed, solutions are sought and the words we here are mostly "economy" and "money."

I am an engineer and this book takes a different approach, the approach engineers take; When we find that something does not work we go back to the models we use and look at them and change the models until what we want to be built is built the way we intended them to be built. Economists and politicians today do not seem to understand that that is how we should react. Or perhaps it is just that they are rich and well-off so that they do not feel the desperate need for change?

If we stop for a moment and look around us and ask us "Why can we live as we do today?" What *exactly* is it that enables us to live as we do today? If we compare the society in Europe, for instance, with the society we had here hundred years ago or a couple of thousand years ago, why can we live differently today? No, it is not the quantity of natural resources. [1] No, it is definitely not the amount of money.

The real reason why our society has changed with time is the accumulated sum of new ideas encapsulated in new technology. Money is in this sense only one small part of new technology, the myriad of ideas and inventions that support our way of living today.

---

[1] For a discussion of this see chapter "Scarce Resources?"

Self-evident you may say. Why then are most solutions and problems formulated in terms where "money" is essential? It is because it is the way we have been taught to think.

Concepts used in economics have become our prison leading us in the wrong direction into a very inhumane world where money is Alpha and Omega. And we do not even see the prison bars that confines us to certain solutions because we think this is just how it must be. We think it is established science. And because we do not see the prison bars but respect them this system of misleading us is so extremely efficient. We become our own wardens.

The models used by economists are not laws of nature and they have most definitely not been handed down by God. The models, ideas and concepts economists use are derived from observations and arguments for how things probably are or ought to be. But that is also exactly how the alternative ideas described in this book have originated.

Of course, in most books about economy a paragraph or even a whole chapter is often devoted to disclosing that the economic concepts taught are not neutral, but that generous confession only makes the theories seem more neutral and trustworthy to the reader! In practice the economic theories and concepts taught are presented and discussed as if they are neutral and unbiased and as such we are not lead to criticize them.

This is why, whether they are liberals, socialists or even communists, politicians tend to choose the same political solutions.

Research done by people such as Professor George Lakoff and professor Robert Cialdini points out a terribly uncomfortable truth: In many ways we function as pre-programmed computers accepting only already established ways of thinking. This book is a politically biased book that believes that this is the main reason why we continue to do the wrong things. We accept unpleasant economic solutions because our human minds have been taught to accept deceptive concepts and economic models as "science."

If we are to change how we think we need new ideas, concepts and models for how we think about economic matters to replace those in use today. And that is in a nutshell what this book is about: This book presents new ways of viewing what is ***true*** wealth and how we can think about this so we can break free from the prison of economic thoughts that today dominates us.

In short, destroy the idea that money represents wealth, that it is the amount of worked time that is the key factor for increasing wealth, point out that the idea of demand and supply often leads to immoral standpoints and so on and we will be enabled to understand that we have been imprisoned. When we realize this we can start shaping new ideas leading to other political solutions and all other good things will follow.

I have no illusion that this little book will transform every Ebenezer Scrooge into an empathic human being. But it does give some arguments to us that want to remain being emphatic human beings and not just soulless components put into some production scheme making the few but smart richer and richer.

Welcome to share my ideas for realizing this dream; a better more emphatic and just world. Read the book, reflect, discuss, contribute your insights and then react!

Everything Begins with Ideas

When we needed to transfer more and more information it was once thought that we would need so much copper cables to transfer all the information that the we would run out of copper. New ideas such as digital transfer of data and the use of glass fibres made that fear laughable. My LCD screen on my table has a larger and better picture, consumes less power, weighs less and costs less than my previous CRT screen. That miracle was made possible by lots of new ideas.

Today we can eat fresh vegetables during all seasons here in Sweden and go to a warmer country in hours. This was impossible a hundred years ago. Today it is possible not because we work more hours but because of new ideas.

Iceboxes were replaced by refrigerators. Our last freezer consumes much less power than the old one and is self-defrosting. New ideas.

Our whole history is a history of how ideas have changed society. New ideas beget new knowledge that changes conditions, sometimes radically. Ideas are like seeds that if properly sawn and cared for can grow into tremendous things and solve problems that we thought could not be solved.

The future is bright for a country that is good at creating new ideas and able to convert them into new products and services.

Self-evident? Obvious? If this is obvious why are newspapers not filled with discussions on how we shall get more ideas and convert these into new products and services? Instead, we find articles on economy about inflation, the rent, unemployment, balanced budgets and so on.

So, we are aware of the impact new ideas have on the society but it is not pointed out. It is not in focus. Its importance is not understood.

It is not only civilian ideas that change society. When the knowledge of how to make cannons came to Europe the whole paradigm of how to construct defences had to change. Defences made of stone-walls could now easily be destroyed.

And still we have not yet tapped into the most powerful ideas; Political and religious ideas have the power to change the whole society in dramatic and far-reaching ways. How would the world look today if the Christian or the Muslim belief systems had not occurred? Or if the communist ideas had not emerged?

Ideas are at the core of every change. Ideas such as the invisible hand of Adam Smith move us or stop us – and mostly without us even being aware of it. Today we are set in a prison of current economic ideas and the purpose of these ideas are to enslave us to the whims and wishes of the very rich. To break free we need new ideas. Why can we not see this obvious fact?

Our Puzzling Inability to See the Obvious

Common sense is not so common. [Voltaire]

In a study of the Canadian federal elections it was found that handsome candidates received many more votes than unattractive candidates. In a follow-up study it was found that voters were unaware of this "In fact, 73 percent of Canadian voters surveyed denied in the strongest possible terms that their votes had been influenced by physical appearance; only 14 percent even allowed for the possibility of such influence." [2]

The awful fact is that we have our strong biases and cemented ways of thinking that make us blind. If we really understood in our hearts that new ideas are the primary reason for increasing true wealth we would not have had this idiotic economy of speculation and this book would never have been written.

But how is it possible that this so very obvious fact of the principal role of new ideas has been and is so ignored? It is possible because of the way the human mind works. Many years ago I was reviewing a software program written in assembler. The designer had used digital filters but it was obvious to me that that was not needed.

---

[2] The psychology of persuasion, Robert B. Cialdini Ph.D., page 171.

The software should do something if the rpm of a motor was above a certain speed and another thing if the rpm was below this speed. Thus a simple `if-then-else` design was the natural choice. Getting some code written in assembler correct using digital filters is very hard! At first the programmer did not understand me but after a while he also saw the obvious and the design was simplified. Why had he programmed using digital filters? He had been working a lot with digital filters in a previous project so his mind was set that way – it was set to use digital filters.

Modern research by people such as Professor George Lakoff and Professor Robert Cialdini confirms clearly that we human beings in many way resemble pre-programmed computers – we follow and continue in the way we have been taught/programmed by previous experience.

When we grow up we accumulate ideas, rules, concepts and so on that make up a framework for how we understand the world. This becomes a classification process for how we should comprehend the events that occur every day. This process goes on automatically in the background of our brains so that "mostly we barely notice that we are even classifying." [3]

That we use an elaborate system of concepts when we think and that we are not usually aware of what concepts we use or how they fit together is "One of the most fundamental results in cognitive science, one that comes from the study of commonsense reasoning." [4] In fact "Most people don't even know that they have conceptual systems, much less how they are structured." [5]

Professor Robert Cialdini adds more understanding to this phenomenon when he refers to the complex information intensive world we live in today. We simply get so much stimulus that we have no way of dealing with it all. We just do not have the time or the capacity to deal with all the impressions we constantly get so we need what he calls shortcuts "we must very often use our stereotypes, our rules of thumb to classify things according to a few key features and

---

[3] Moral politics, by George Lakoff. Page 162.
[4] Moral politics, by George Lakoff. Page 4.
[5] Moral politics, by George Lakoff. Page 388.

then to respond mindlessly when one or another of these trigger features is present." [6]

An example may clarify the idea of shortcuts. Recently I bought a pair of new spectacles. I wanted them to be lightweight so I choose plastic lenses and spectacle frames of titanium as I have done before – thinking this would give me a lightweight pair of spectacles. But when I got them I found out that their weight was about double that of my old pair of spectacles. I had "forgotten" to check that the spectacle frames were not thicker. I used the shortcut:

$$plastic\ lenses + frames\ of\ titanium = lightweight\ spectacles$$

Stupid? Yes, but that illustrates how our minds function. We look at some selected key features and then further analysis stops dead. This is exactly what happens when we are presented with economic "science." Analysis stops dead and we accept the solutions presented to us because they fit what we have been previously taught.

The use of shortcuts is basically good for us since it sets the human mind free to concentrate on other things and there are a lot of things for the human mind to deal with in our hectic society. However, when this behaviour is taken the next step to how we accept or not accept things depending on what we have been taught about economy we arrive at a very uncomfortable conclusion; You or I may be a red communist or a dark blue conservative, but *if we have gone to the same economic schools we have been brainwashed in the same way so we think in the same way*. That is, we have been taught to trigger on the same key features!

And most ugly of all, we do this even if we do not want to because we are unaware of this phenomenon! We are locked in our static bookkeeping way of viewing production and what wealth is because of what we have been taught.

Economists may think they are good people doing good things to make the economy work well or fix things with all their economic

---

[6] The psychology of persuasion, Robert B. Cialdini Ph.D., page 7.

concepts but in the end they lead us astray because they have become blind and do not recognize that the sole source of new wealth are new ideas.

To set us free from this taught static way of viewing economy in terms of money we have to break free from these economic ideas that bind us to the current unproductive economic framework way of thinking.

And that is in itself the basic idea of this book. An idea that can, if it becomes understood and accepted by people, revolutionize our society.

Let the economists talk about price, demand and supply, price, that we should work more hours to ensure our wealth and then that damned parameter price again. But we should instead have as our canon the role of new ideas. Or stated in another way, the fundamental role of new and better technology to enable us to create more true wealth.

Summary

We stated the obvious but forgotten fundamental role of new ideas as the source of change in a society.

We also discussed several indications from research that show how difficult it is for us to change how we interpret things. I may be a red communist or a dark blue conservative, but if I have gone to the same economic schools as others I have been brainwashed in the same way as others and I think in the same way. And most ugly of all, I will be unaware of this phenomenon!

If we really understood in our hearts that new ideas – new technology – is the primary reason for increasing true wealth we would not have had this idiotic economy of speculation that we see again and again through history and this book would never have had to be written.

Wealth or True Wealth?

To call forth a concept a word is needed; to portray a phenomenon, a concept is needed. All three mirror one and the same reality. [Antoine Laurent Lavoisier]

This book is about creating true wealth in our nations rather than just wealth. We want wealth that represents things that are usable to us and that has been created under fair trade conditions.

Nobel Prize winner Muhammad Yunus sets the stage for our drama well when he points out that capitalism has created a one-dimensional human being with one goal: To maximize profits. This has cut us off from other aspects of life such as religious, emotional and political aspects. When we follow the simple idea "that you are contributing to the society and the world in the best possible manner if you just concentrate on squeezing out the maximum for yourself" [7] we often find that things do not look to good around us. We then try to ignore this and blame it on market failures because well-functioning markets should just not give us unpleasant results!

Muhammad Yunus continues "I think things are going wrong not because of "market failure." It is much deeper than that. . . . it is the failure to capture the essence of a human being in our theory. . . . Their emotions, beliefs, priorities, behaviour patterns . . ."

Muhammad Yunus is here criticising the idea that dominates economic thought of today; The myth that started with Adam Smith, the idea of the "invisible hand" which has been encapsulated in the idea of the economic man, homo economicus; a human with a rational judgment based on being perfectly informed that in self-interest goes for wealth and avoids labor if possible.

In his book the *Wealth of Nations* Adam Smith holds forth that the free market, while appearing chaotic and unrestrained, is actually guided to produce the right amount and variety of goods by this "invisible hand." Smith believed that while human motives were often

---

[7] Social Business Entrepreneurs Are the Solution, Muhammad Yunus. Nobel Prize winner. http://www.social-business-entrepreneur.com/ (2010-05-28).

driven by selfishness and greed, the competition in the free market would tend to benefit society as a whole by keeping prices low, while still building in an incentive for a wide variety of goods and services. The idea can be summarized with this quote from the book *Wealth of Nations*:

> "It is not from the benevolence of the butcher, the brewer, or the baker that we expect our dinner, but from their regard to their own interest. We address ourselves, not to their humanity but to their self-love, and never talk to them of our own necessities but of their advantages."

This is the gospel of self-interest, the belief that we can be selfish trying to maximize income for ourselves and this will by this invisible hand maximize the total revenue of society as a whole. This near religious belief has today become a one way ticket away from empathy and common sense.

It is of course a belief that is in stark contrast to what is believed in the great churches. "Do good and the Kingdom of God will be realized in our midst, act according to self-interest and the world will be destroyed, says Benedict XVI." [8]

What we need instead of this semi-religious belief in self-interest are models based on established practices of how to build models as done in established fields of science such as physics. Interesting to note is that not even Adam Smith had the simplified semi-religious belief the way this model has become used by the conservatives today to justify their greed and selfish behaviour.

Noam Chomsky points out [9] that Adam Smith was well aware of the maxim "All for ourselves, and nothing for other people, seems, in every age of the world, to have been the vile maxim of the masters of mankind." [10] And that Adam Smith understood that the invisible hand would destroy the possibility of a decent human existence "unless government takes pains to prevent" this outcome, as must be assured

---

[8] Zenit News Agency, 11/25/2008 "Self-Interest Will Destroy the World."

[9] Notes of NAFTA: "The Masters of Man," Noam Chomsky, The Nation, March, 1993.

[10] Book III, Chapter IV, pg.448.

in "every improved and civilized society." It will destroy community, the environment and human values generally -- and even the masters themselves, which is why the business classes have regularly called for state intervention to protect them from market forces.

If we are to avoid the current trend of worshipping the "invisible hand" so we can avoid having it "destroy the possibility of a decent human existence" we need a major change in how we think.

Thomas Kuhn used the term **paradigm shift** to describe changes in *our basic assumptions* within the ruling theory of science. Figure 1 illustrates this idea. When the present state of established knowledge is unable to meet our needs, we encounter a crisis. This crisis is followed by a revolution greatly changing the established knowledge, that is, our way of doing/modeling/understanding something. After such a paradigm shift our way of viewing the world has changed dramatically.

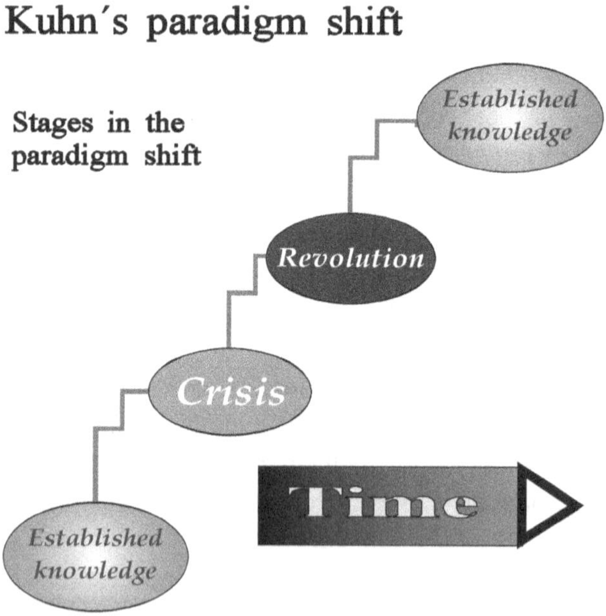

Kuhn´s paradigm shift

Figure 1 Kuhn's paradigm shift.

Our changing perception of our universe is a good example of this principle. When the idea of having the earth as the center resulted in too complex models, the model was eventually replaced by one where the sun was at the center instead. When not even this was enough to explain astronomical observations, the sun lost its role as center and we had a model much closer to the one we use today.

Does sound like a good idea does it not to have a paradigm shift if we want to get away from this crazy world of economic speculation, bubbles and starvation among people does it not?

What will a new paradigm shift involve? We will next perform some experiments to highlight the difference between wealth, represented by money, and true wealth. How does our comprehension of wealth need to be changed?

Three Radical Experiments

> *The beginning is the most important part of the work.*
> [Plato]

In experiment number 1 we write down how much money we have. That is, we make a list of how many banknotes, coins, shares we have and what we have in bank accounts and funds. All the paper money, coins and sums we have stored as numbers in computers are listed. Then we destroy all that we have listed but keep the lists. We burn the banknotes, dump the coins somewhere deep in the ocean and delete all numbers in the memories of computers indicating how much we had in shares and so on. Whew! What shall we do now? Well, assuming we are all honest, we can now start the printing presses and print new banknotes to distribute among us and simply insert the numbers in our computers again. Replacing the coins will take some more work and it will all be quite some work but we will survive.

In experiment number 2 we keep all that was destroyed in experiment 1. Instead we destroy all the buildings we have (except those housing our banknotes, backup tapes with our numbers indicating how much shares we have and so on), the roads are destroyed, our clothes are burnt (how embarrassing!), all the food and machinery and everything else that has been built by human beings except the banknotes and the things destroyed in experiment number 1 are now totally eradicated from the surface of the earth.

Now this is a much bigger problem than in experiment 1 do you not agree? Now, it is doubtful if even half of us will even survive because we have money but nothing to buy or rent. What shall we eat? Where shall we live?

If you find experiment 2 ridiculous because we would never do such a thing, just think about that third very big world war that we were/are so afraid of. It would do about the same thing.

And it gets worse, when after a hundred years or so our society has been restored it is time for experiment no 3. This time we start by doing exactly as in experiment 2 but this time we also take a pill that has been sent to us from a civilisation somewhere in the universe that is deeply interested in these experiments. This pill makes us forget all the knowledge we had such as technical knowledge, knowledge of how to read and write and all that the human society has learnt and stored as information including novels and other books during the last couple of thousands of years. We do get some new knowledge imparted to us through these pills though, the knowledge of how to hunt and make fire for instance. This time most of us will die and it will take at least a couple of thousands of years to get back to the type of civilisation we have today.

Now, what is all this about? Well, you see:

- In experiment number 1 we destroyed wealth,
- in experiment number 2 we destroyed true wealth, and
- in experiment number 3 we destroyed true wealth and technology.

And that is the theme of this book, the difference between wealth and true wealth and how technology is the fundamental enabler of true wealth. The shift in focus is a shift from thinking in money terms to a focus on how technology can enable us to create true wealth. And from this change in focus all true good things will follow.

Summary

In this chapter we set the theme for this book, how new ideas – new technology – is the fundamental enabler of true wealth. We also noted that we think as we have been taught. The ideas we have been taught act as a filter or a prison making it very difficult to see other solutions than what this filter allow us to see. We thus need to discover new ideas so we can see things in new perspectives if we are going to want to and be able to change things but this will be hard work since we will tend to resist these new ideas.

But this work is worth the time and effort we spend – we do want a better more emphatic society do we not?

In the Beginning

> *"In the beginning God created the heavens and the earth ."*
> *[Genesis 1:1]*

> *"Then God said, "I give you every seed-bearing plant on*
> *the face of the whole earth and every tree that has fruit with*
> *seed in it. They will be yours for food." [Genesis 1:29]*

In the beginning there was no money. There was no need for it but
man soon fell from this paradisiacal state and found a need to
exchange things with each other. Someone had salt and someone else
had skin so people started to barter. This was a bit inconvenient so
people came up with ideas of using standard items in exchange like
pieces of gold or silver or even peppercorns, shells or whatever took
the fancy.

The first type of money was born: **Commodity money**. This is a
type of money where the material itself is the money. We have a one-
to-one relationship; the commodity itself constitutes the money, and
the money is the commodity. You had salt and sold it, got your
peppercorns, and could then rather easily use these peppercorns as
payment for a piece of skin or something else you wanted by just
paying the "price" set on the other commodity you wanted. Of course
some barter often took place in order to change the set price.

Development continued and slabs of metal became nice coins of
gold and other metals. This was still a type of honest money as long as
the gold in the coin was gold and had not been tampered with. The
money (if not tampered with) represented a piece of wealth that was
used to barter for another type of wealth but in a more formalized and
efficient way.

Travelling around with such valuable things as commodity money
was inconvenient and dangerous so the idea of *using something that
could represent the money* was invented and **representative money**
was born. This money can also be in the form of coins but more often
in the form of paper such as banknotes. This is also a type of honest
money since it is supposed to be exchangeable for a fixed quantity of

commodities, typically gold. If it cannot be exchanged in a direct and fixed relation to some commodity which backs it we talk about fraud. We can call these two types of **honest money** for **barter money**.

honest money = barter money
*   = commodity money + representative money*

These two types of money are honest because they cannot cheat us since they have or represent an **intrinsic** [11] value not dependant on anything else but itself. Or as Gottfried Wilhelm Leibniz put it *"Two things are identical if one can be substituted for the other without affecting the truth."*

Well, work is often difficult and if we steal outright we may get into problems with the authorities. So what do we do? We invent new ways of getting more money without producing anything. Usury soon became popular. Aristotle [12] formulated the classical view against usury:

> "it doesn't beget more money the way cows beget more cows. "Money exists not by nature but by law": "The most hated sort (of wealth getting) and with the greatest reason, is usury, which makes a gain out of money itself and not from the natural object of it. For money was intended to be used in exchange but not to increase at interest. And this term interest (tokos), which means the birth of money from money Is applied to the breeding of money because the offspring resembles the parent. Wherefore of all modes of getting wealth, this is the most unnatural." (1258b POLITICS)

And Aristotle especially disliked usurers:

> "...those who ply sordid trades, pimps and all such people, and those who lend small sums at high rates. For all these take more than they ought, and from the wrong sources. What is

---

[11] Intrinsic, belonging to a thing by its very nature.
[12] 384-322 BC.

common to them is evidently a sordid love of gain..." [1122a, ETHICS]

Indeed, what we see today in the financial world is that not a sordid love of gain?

> "He lends at usury and takes excessive interest. Will such a man live? He will not! Because he has done all these detestable things, he will surely be put to death and his blood will be on his own head." [Ezekiel 18:13]

Aristotle understood that money was sterile something many of us do not quite understand today. It is as if we believe that in the morning the banknotes and coins wake up, eat their breakfast and off they go to companies, singing "Hey ho let's go," and there this working capital toil all day producing things.

Today money is a sweeping term that refers to anything that *can operate as money* and then I do not mean operate honestly as with barter money. In economics the term **financial instrument is** often used for things that can "operate as money." Financial instruments are in their turn divided into cash instruments and derivative instruments. It is nearly possible to understand what a cash instrument is because it is something whose value is determined by some market. The interested reader is referred to the internet or some other place for a detailed description of derivative instruments.

Let's talk a little more about money though. We have **credit money** which is a claim against someone that can be used for the purchase of things. We have **fiat** [13] **money** which is actually also credit money but is more proud because it is declared by a government to be acceptable and officially recognized as payment for all debts, both public and private. That is, the government can just say that now dear members of the society this is just how it is so you better obey and think the money is worth something. This is the type of money we use today and it works quite well all the time up until the

---

[13] Fiat: an arbitrary decree or pronouncement, esp. by someone - like a government - that have absolute authority to enforce it.

day too many people lose faith in it and start to regard paper money as, well, as paper.

Things have become very complicated indeed. Especially since people working in the financial sector became very inventive and started to develop new ideas such as the derivatives (mentioned above) and "futures," "forwards," "options" and "swaps." Just look these words up and try to understand what it is all about. And in the unlikely case that you will understand what it is all about go on and look up "hedging," "speculation and arbitrage," "OTC and exchange traded," "bilateral netting," "gross negative fair value," "notional amount," "perpetual preferred shareholders equity."

That last is a beauty. It sounds as something from an old B science fiction film. *"Hey guys, we crashed on the planet because the 'derivative bilateral netting trust gyrator' had a 'perpetual preferred shareholders equity' problem."*

Well, these are just some of the imaginative concepts used in the financial sector to acquire money without creating anything new in the real world – like a new machine, or more potatoes.

So what do we do? Spend the rest of our lifetime collecting doctoral degrees in economics so we can fool ourselves that this is OK and perhaps even that it is usable? No, faced with this impenetrable complexity we must show the same brilliant daring as Alexander the Great showed when he faced the Gordian knot. After having tried to untie the knot but failed as all others before him had failed he was different. He stepped back, drew his sword, and in one powerful stroke severed the knot. If we do this with this confusion of economic terms, models and concepts we arrive at this formula:

The money in a system = barter money plus bubble money

Yes, that is right folks, we actually have something of worth because it is honest so we can barter with it because of its intrinsic value or because it represents something such, or we have something invented to fool us we have more than we have, a bubble. The essence of this formula is found in this quote:

"He who has been stealing must steal no longer, but must work, doing something useful with his own hands, that he may have something to share with those in need." [Eph 4:28, NIV]

If we are hungry we do **not** need a banknote, we need a hamburger or a pizza. We need something we can eat, not money because we cannot eat money. Did that ring true to you or did you immediately think that the banknote was OK too? Why? If we are hungry there is no intrinsic value in a banknote that can stop our hunger. There is such intrinsic value in a hamburger. If you do not follow me here please go back to chapter *Three Radical Experiments* found earlier in the book because this point is very important.

Summary

We have honest money that we can use when we barter because it either has an intrinsic value in itself that makes it attractive or because it represents something such. That is, commodity money or representative money.

Or, we have something else, we have something that is not worth anything in itself and does not represent anything of worth. This bubble money can only be used to barter with if we are fooled into believing it is worth something.

Enter some Mathematics

The Language of Mathematics

There is no need to panic because the word mathematics is mentioned. Mathematics is just another language created by mathematicians because they want to express things in as short a way as possible.

There is a darker side to mathematics though. Many people want to use mathematics to express their views because it makes their views more convincing. To understand this phenomenon we relate a story from Professor Robert Cialdinis book *Influence*. It is about a study where "men who saw a new-car ad that included a seductive female model rated the car as faster, more appealing, more expensive-looking, and better-designed than did men who viewed the same ad without the model." [14] Of course the men refused to believe that the presence of the young woman had influenced their judgments. It is a well known fact that we as human beings utterly refuse to believe in facts that are insulting to us.

This is an example of what Robert Cialdini calls the "Liking" effect. Converted to the world of mathematics it translates into this: If you can express your subjective ideas and opinions in the language of mathematics your ideas will sound like science and take on the presumed objectivity of science. Your subjective opinions expressed in the mathematical language will then have a much greater impact on the audience.

However, economics is far from the real science of physics where we do find simple and repeatable natural events that are suitable to describe with the language of mathematics. So dressing subjective views of events taken from our extremely complex and confusing world of human interactions in the language of mathematics is mostly a clever trick. It is using the phenomenon that you can transfer positive traits by the "Liking" effect. That is, just like the presence of that young model in the car influenced the men we will be influenced by the use of mathematics. And of course, just as the men refused to

---

[14] Influence, science and practice, Robert B. Cialdini Ph.D., page 161.

admit that they were influenced I guess most economists will refuse to admit what they are doing; That what they are actually doing is expressing **their** ideas and arguments using the language of mathematics. However, views and opinions of course remain just that even if they are expressed in the language of mathematics.

Well, to be fair there are other reasons to use mathematics than to give credibility to your ideas. Translating your ideas and opinions into mathematics makes it possible to express things in a very concise and precise way and it also often makes it much easier to combine ideas to describe new ideas and come to conclusions.

By showing that we can also express **our** ideas and argument using mathematics we should find ourselves in a better position to combat the ideas and arguments of the economists. So let's add some mathematical flavour to our text.

The Sum of

We had this formula:

The money in a system = barter money plus bubble money

By introducing the + sign we make our plain English a little bit more mathematical:

The money in a system = barter money + bubble money

This formula can be made even more mathematical by introducing the symbol $\sum$.

$$\sum_{all} money = \sum_{all} barter\ money + \sum_{all} bubble\ money$$

These expressions state the same thing but in the last one we have converted our English phrase into mathematics by using the symbol $\sum$. $\sum$ just means "the sum of."

The "all" under the symbol indicates what we sum over. That is, we sum all the "whatever it is we sum" in the system. Thus, this equation just says, the sum of all money is equal to the sum of all barter money plus all the bubble money.

Functions

In this book we use functions to express in a concise way dependencies between things; Formulas that express relations between things.

Say that we want to express the opinion that the number of hours we work is related to our income. Then we could express it this way:

$$income = f(H) \text{ [US\$]}$$

This means, our income is a function *f*, of the hours *H* we work and we measure it in US\$. *H* is an input to the function and is called an argument. [15]

Note, this does not in itself say that the more hours we work the higher would our income be. If we wanted to add that information we could express it like this:

$$income = f(H), \; f'(H) > 0 \text{ [16]}$$

The last part, *f'(H,)* is called a derivate. If it is positive, it indicates that if *H* increases so does *f*, that is our income.

In economics we can find the following equation which is used to express the view that a nation's growth competitiveness depends on three things:

$$GC_i = f(T_i, PI_i, ME_i)$$

Where:

$GC_i = Growth\ Competitiveness$
$T_i = Technology$

---

[15] To avoid confusion with the more general usage of the word "argument" I will often refer to such input arguments simply as "inputs."

[16] The symbol > means greater than.

$PI_i = Public\ Institutions$
$ME_i = Macroeconomic\ Environment$

In this case the "rule" for finding a value for $f(T_i, PI_i, ME_i)$ is of course very complex and must be determined by analysis and discussions and no direct generally usable equation is available. However, note, that even if we have no easily described rule we can use this notation to make statements. We can express our view, summarize our argument, using this notation. That is, in this case we argue that a nation's competitiveness (GC) depends on:

- The technology (T) used in the development process.
- The state of the country's public institutions (PI). (It is argued that the quality of public institutions affects the efficiency).
- The quality of the macroeconomic environment (ME).

Of course, if you do not agree with the views summarized by the functions we use there is nothing that demands that you have to accept them! Views and opinions even if expressed in the language of mathematics remain views and opinions. Not every economist understands this. But we must understand it!

You can find more information about functions in *Appendix, More about Functions.*

Trealth

> *The whole of science is nothing more than a refinement of everyday thinking. [Albert Einstein]*

In the beginning (just after Genesis 1:29) the only things we had to barter with were the things we had just in front of us, the fruits and other plants etc. Everything that was useful for us were there just for the taking of it and all those things indeed had an intrinsic value. That was the wealth that existed. Now, let's connect to the idea of utilitarianism.

> **Utilitarianism** is the idea that the worth of an action is determined by its contribution to overall utility, that is, its contribution to happiness or pleasure as summed among all persons. Sometimes this is measured in a unit called [util] or [utils].

We steal this idea of utilitarianism and adapt it to mean that what is worth something is worth something because it contributes something good to us. It is something utilitarian we want such as a fruit, some wood or a computer for instance. It is also something others want (not everybody but enough of them) to give it some barter power. Wealth in some form thus. The term wealth is however misleading because it actually is interpreted as money by a lot of people. Think about that. You can even read that in many dictionaries! This is not what we mean here at all with wealth.

So to avoid the mistake of thinking that for instance a large stack of 1000 US$ banknotes is wealth we will use the term **trealth** instead of the term wealth because we want to speak about true wealth and not just wealth. True wealth, trealth. Just think about Daffy Duck trying to say wealth eating a couple of hot dogs and the term trealth will stick forever in your mind.

After all, who wants a large stack of 1000 US$ banknotes? They can at the most be used to help build a fire or in an emergency be used in the bathroom for a not so noble but quite necessary thing. But toilet paper is so much better for that use. And of course if that amount of money exists solely as some figures in a computer in some bank it cannot even be used in an emergency visit to the bathroom.

So what exactly is true wealth, trealth? Basically trealth are all the things that we want to have. This would then of course include products and services that we want to have but it could also include things such as, peace, a nature in balance and many other things. We would also have to put some limiting rule that there should be a minimal consensus about what to include. In this book, however, for practical reasons I will take a more traditional products and service perspective and leave other aspects out of discussion in most cases.

Ok, what trealth did we have in the beginning? Well, we had the fruits, the wood etc:

$$trealth = sum\ of\ the\ fruits, plants\ etc\ [Genesis\ style]$$

Remembering that the symbol $\sum$ just meant "the sum of" we get:

$$trealth = \sum_{all} fruits, plants\ etc$$

And sometimes someone was able to catch a fish and we get this formula:

$$trealth = \sum_{all} fruits, plants\ etc\ ...\ and\ a\ few\ fish$$

How much trealth did we have? Well as much as we could pick up. The more hours we worked the more we could pick up or catch. We can say that trealth was a function of how many hours we worked and that can be expressed like this:

$$trealth = f(\sum_{community} hours\ worked),$$
$$(the\ more\ hours\ worked, the\ more\ we\ get)$$

(And of course, you remember that f just meant a function, a formula expressing a relation between things). Which here means that trealth is a function f of how many hours we as a community spent on picking that nice looking fruit and how much time we spent splashing around in the water trying to catch fish. We can make this shorter by introducing "H" like this:

$$H = \sum_{community} hours\ worked$$

Using this "H" we now get this formula which is more beautiful to mathematicians because it is shorter:

$$trealth = f(H), \qquad (the\ more\ hours\ worked, the\ more\ we\ get)$$

The last part can be expressed using a derivate and lets add our unit of measurement:

$$trealth = f(H), \quad f'(H) > 0 \quad [util]$$

That is, the amount of trealth – how much *util* – that we can produce depends on the hours we work [$trealth = f(H)$] and that if we work more hours we get more trealth [$f'(H) > 0$].

    Hardly had any time gone by and someone got the idea to use a fishing net and suddenly we could catch more fish! And that was not all. People started to settle down so they could saw and reap large harvests of cereals such as wheat, corn, oats and other edible grain. How much we could accumulate was now not only a function of how many hours we worked. New ideas made it possible to produce more each hour. Imagine!

Summary

Trealth are all the things that we want to have. In this book we for practical reasons most of the time limit trealth to mean all the services and products that we want to have and we measure these in the unit [*util*].

Trealth and Technology

> *Man is a tool-using animal. . . Without tools he is nothing,*
> *with tools he is all. [Thomas Carlyle]*

Technology

Perhaps the most common of the economic intrinsic theories of values is the one connected to the labor theory of value that says that the value of an item comes from the amount of labor spent producing the item. For instance, if something can be produced by five workers in 10 hours each then that something is worth 5 x 10 = 50 man-hours.

This sounds exactly as what we suggested in the previous chapter where we stated the view that trealth was a function of how many hours we work:

$$trealth = f(H), \ f'(H) > 0 \ [util]$$

Now if things just were that simple! Because, then we could increase trealth by just working slower or more inefficient so that it would take more hours to complete some work. Abhorrent idea! Not all worked hours are equal. Enter technology:

> **Technology** is the application of knowledge for practical ends, a technological process, invention, or method. In short, the sum of the ways in which social groups provides themselves with the material objects and other nice things of their civilization.

With the word technology we will in this book mean all ideas *that enables the creation of trealth* so imagination, knowledge and information is also included in this enabling factor for creation of trealth. The way we run companies, resolve conflicts and get along when we produce products and services are also included in technology. Viewed from this perspective money is just another idea adding to the sum of technology we use.

It could be argued that there are other important enablers than ideas for trealth such as safety, low corruption and so on but in order to limit the scope of discussion I will not include such aspects in this book however important they are. Because trealth are things that we truly want to have, technology for war may not necessarily be included! Because we focus on technology as an encapsulation of ideas that enable us to create more true wealth we can use this simple definition of technology:

> **Technology** are all the ideas we have collected and systematized that *enable* us to provides ourselves with trealth, that is all the nice things we want to have in our society.

The emergence of technology is a dynamic and fascinating process. Not only did we go from being hunters always on the move to settled down prosperous farmers, so we could saw and reap great harvests of grain but one day someone invented the idea of the plow which made it possible to get even larger harvests. Well, not all farmers were prosperous, even at those early times. Schemes, concepts and reasons are constantly being invented to make sure some people get more of the nice things than others. Often some got much more – just like today.

Anyway, then someone invented an even better plow and someone else got the idea that we could put an ox in front of the plow so we did not have to drag it ourselves. Time passes by and we get a reaping-machine and then a combine-harvester. The story goes on and thousands and millions of ideas are born that make life a bit easier and nicer. We sit in a cold cave without light or warmth. Someone gets the idea and the daring to steal fire from a burning tree after it has been struck with lightning. Well, I was not there but that is what they taught us in school.

Then someone makes a candle, the kerosene lamp appears, Edison invents the electric bulb which was the result of testing many thousands of ideas until he found one that worked. Then came the low energy lamp. A lamp that does not only shine as good as the electric bulb but also uses much fewer watts for this and to top it, also lasts longer. And now we see the led lamp coming that shines at even fewer watts and lasts even longer! These are certainly usable ideas. Things of use are the things we want so surely they must also represent trealth, true wealth. Do you not emphatically agree with that?

Now these things, the electric bulb and so on can be called commodities because a **commodity** is an article of trade or commerce, a product as distinguished from a service, something of use, advantage, or value, any unprocessed or partially processed good, as a grain, fruit or vegetable, or a precious metal and so forth.

New ideas – new technology – are the thing that makes it possible for us to get 1) more and 2) better things to barter with. A hundred years ago nobody could go to the Canary Islands from Sweden in a couple of hours and few could get fresh tomatoes in the winter. Most people lived in small often dark and cold houses and had to work six or seven days a week at twelve hours or more. Nobody could watch movies, listen to music at will with the same ease and quality as today at home or get news shown on TV. And these examples are only a few examples from a very long list. The sum of different commodities and services has not only grown but also grown in quantity and quality. Why? Because the amount of hours worked per person has increased? No. It is because we have accumulated more and better ideas.

Exactly what has happened? And how will it affect our formula? In a big way! We can see that trealth depends on technology:

$$T = \sum_{all} idea_i * k_i \ [technic]$$

The ideas we sum here could be patents or ideas expressed in some more general way that has a positive impact on the amount of trealth in a country. A more exact estimate would demand a lot of study and become an approximation anyway just like estimates of growth competitiveness (GC)[17]. Luckily this is not necessary because the general conclusion that T increases with the sum of ideas should be quite obvious to the reader. Well, perhaps not if you happen to be a politician or economist but such people will probably not read this book anyway. And if they read this book they would probably get a

---

[17] See Appendix, More about Functions.

stroke because they so love the idea that money is the solution and source of all good things – not ideas.

Well, back to the equation! The reason for the k_i multiplier is that it is probable that the worth of ideas differ in their ability to increase trealth in a community.

In the same way as a unit has been invented for the utilitarian value that trealth represents ([util]) we can have a unit for T which we call [technic]. Adding H for worked hours

$$H = \Sigma_{community} \ hours \ worked_i \ [hour]$$

And using T we can express our argument with this concise formula:

$$trealth = f(H,T) \ [util]$$

Yes, you guessed correctly. This expresses the view that the (sum of) trealth in a community is a function f of how many "hours that has been spent on work by each person in community" and "the sum of all ideas that exist" in the same community.

The equation $trealth = f(H,T)$ is of course a functional description at a very high level. It does not say anything about how this function $f(H,T)$ depends on the inputs H and T. It is even possible that the more hours we work the less trealth we get. For instance, if we are programming very late and happen to introduce stupid solutions because we are tired or just destroy the code or if we are engaging in war and destroy things.

However, if we do want to say that our function $f(H,T)$ increases with some inputs, such as H and T, in a mathematical way, we can do it like this: [18]

$$\frac{\partial f(H,T)}{\partial h} > 0, \qquad \frac{\partial f(H,T)}{\partial t} > 0$$

The first expresses the view that the more hours we work the more trealth we get and the second says the same for technology. These two

---

[18] The symbol > means greater than.

added elements are called (partial) derivatives and they indicate what happens with a function, in this case our $f(T, H)$, when we make a small change. If a derivative is positive, that is greater than zero as is the case here, this indicates that if we add a little amount of H or T, respectively, the function will also increase in value. [19]

Because we cannot be certain that increasing H will increase the function but we are quite sure, when we look back on the historical development, that new and better ideas increases trealth, we can at least confidently express this view:

$$trealth = f(H,T), \qquad \frac{\partial f(H,T)}{\partial t} > 0$$

Bubble Money and Barter Money

We earlier had this formula for trealth:

$$trealth = \sum_{all} fruits, plants\ etc\ \dots\ and\ a\ few\ fish$$

Using a more modern formula where we also regard services as something we want and use the word commodity we get this formula:

$$trealth = \sum_{all} available\ commodities, services - that\ we\ want$$

This is equal to this even more mathematical looking formula:

$$trealth = \sum_{all,wanted} commodity_i + \sum_{all,wanted} service_i$$

Where we thus sum over all available commodities (but only those things we want, those that have a utilitarian value to us). That is:

---

[19] As mentioned, earlier. An equation *trealth* = *f(H,T)* only states that *f* is a function that depends on *H* and *T*. It does not automatically say that the more of *H* and *T* respectively we have the more *f* we get. Because we here argue that this is true, that is, increasing *H* and/or *T* in this case, will increase *f(H,T)* we can express this argument by using these partial derivatives and stating that they are greater than zero.

$$\sum_{all,wanted} commodity_i = commodity_1 + commodity_2 + commodity_3$$
$$+ commodity_4 + \cdots.$$

And the same for services:

$$\sum_{all,wanted} service_i = service_1 + service_2 + service_3 + service_4 + \cdots.$$

If we wanted to include the more general perspective that trealth is all the things we want including peace, a nature in balance, work environments that are good for the workers and so on we would have to add a third term to our equation above and we get:

$$trealth = \sum_{all,wanted} commodity_i$$
$$+ \sum_{all,wanted} service_i + \sum_{all,wanted} other\ things_i \ ^{20}$$

Please note that for practical reasons I will leave out the third term in the following discussion about trealth.

It now becomes important to point out that the "f" in $f(H,T)$ does **not** stand for "function." The "f" is the **name** of the function. Thus we can also have functions such as $commodities(H,T)$ and $services(H,T)$ or sticking to the mathematical love for short notations we can use $c(H,T)$ and $s(H,T)$. These would then be two functions called "c" and "s" where "c" refers to commodities and "s" refers to services respectively. Simple is it not? The "(H,T)" means that the value of each such commodity or service depends on how

---

[20] All these sums would then sum [util] values. The equation is here presented at a high level of abstraction and we would not only in an actual summation have to come to some agreement on how much [util] something represents but also have to decide if we should perform the summation at a level of single instances or as groups. For instance, if cars represent util values typically between 10 and 30, should we sum all cars ($22 + 12 + 25 + 11 \ldots$) or should we sum them as a group (1 million cars times some average value, say 16)?

many hours (H) that has been worked to get it and the technological level (T).

$$c(H,T) = \sum_{all,wanted} commodity_i = \sum_{a,w} commodity_i$$

$$s(H,T) = \sum_{all,wanted} service_i = \sum_{a,w} service_i$$

The "a, w" is our short notation that the summing should be done on all available items that are wanted items. Combining these with our earlier function for trealth we get:

$$trealth = \sum_{a,w} commodity_i + \sum_{a,w} service_i = c(H,T) + s(H,T)$$

Each of these things we sum are things that we want and that have an **intrinsic** barter value and all things that have an intrinsic barter value is entitled to be or to be represented by a barter money item. We introduce the **barter function**:

$$b(some\ input\ util) = some\ money$$

The function $b()$ is a barter function that converts inputs of [util] values to output in some currency of money. Naturally it is assumed that $b'() > 0$. That is, the more util, the more money $b()$ should be output. Using this we make this **definition** of barter money:

$$\sum_{all} barter\ money_i = \sum_{a,w} b(commodity_i) + \sum_{a,w} b(service_i)$$

This means that for every commodity and service that we value by setting a [util] value on it there should be some barter money for it. That is, for everything we value in society such as roads, bridges, houses, different needed services and so forth we agree that we can have some corresponding money for it. We introduced the following equation in chapter *The Sum of*:

$$\sum_{all} money = \sum_{all} barter\ money + \sum_{all} bubble\ money$$

The first thing we can note using this equation is that if there were no bubble money the money we use in a society would all be barter money. That is if:

$$\sum_{all} bubble\ money = 0$$

Then:

$$\sum_{all} money = \sum_{all} barter\ money$$

An alternative **definition** of barter money could thus be:

> If there is no bubble money in use in a society then the sum of barter money equals the sum of money used.

That is, if money can only be added when something of barter value is created then we will only have barter money. Of course, also, if things of barter value are destroyed the corresponding barter money must be withdrawn.

If we combine the earlier equation defining barter money with the equation relating money, barter money and bubble money we can write:

$$\sum_{all} money = \sum_{a,w} b(commodity_i) + \sum_{a,w} b(service_i)$$
$$+ \sum_{all} bubble\ money\ [21]$$

This is the same as we said above. When considering all money directly such as in banknotes or the more mystical types represented by all these complex new economic concepts "that operate as money" we have honest money that corresponds to existing commodities and existing services and dishonest bubble money.

If we apply this equation to a person or an organisation such as a company we can see that there are basically two ways of increasing the sum of money they have (the left most side of the equation). We can either:

1. Increase the sum of commodities and/or services that have an intrinsic barter value, or
2. We can increase the sum of bubble money.

How can we increase the sum of bubble money? I see several ways bubble money can be created:

1. **Direct**. We start our printing presses pouring out new banknotes and coins. (Only good for countries, otherwise it is illegal).
2. **Money created by banks**. Most of us believe banks only lend out money that has been entrusted to them by depositors. In fact, banks can create additional money from issued loans using the loans as assets. (See chapter *The Fractional Reserve System*.)
3. **Magic money**. Issuing things that can be used – operate – as money. For instance a company issuing new shares. These then act as a sort of money because they can be exchanged for other things such as bank notes. **Very magic money**. That is, derivatives and all the other hard to understand forms of financial instruments going all the way from the fantastic to the very bizarre.

---

[21] That the index *i* is not shown in one summation does not make the summations functionally different. Setting out the *i* is just showing some more details.

All these ways increase the amount of money available for spending on things but without anything happening in the real world. Nothing is created that has a real intrinsic barter value that corresponds to the increase of money. This means that prices of for instances houses and apartments can now soar to new heights!

This is often referred to as **money creation** and is the reason why the market pressure and smart marketing can be used to increase the prices of houses and apartments. Because if there was no extra money "created" smart brokers would have a difficult time making the price go up by using "styling" and other techniques because there would not be any new money to support the new higher prices!

The idea of "creating" money is of course a tempting idea. That way we can get more wealth so very easily but as we all should understand, it leads to inflation or if we work really hard at pumping in new money in a system, it leads to hyperinflation such as in Germany after world war one or in Zimbabwe in modern times. We are all very curious about how much inflation all the money that has been pumped into the US economic system will give us and when. We live in exciting times!

The Fractional Reserve System

Let's look a little closer at one of these ways of creating new money, the **fractional reserve system**. It is a way for banks to loan out more money than has been deposited in them. This creation of new money is made possible by the fractional reserve system which is the banking practice in which banks keep only a fraction of their deposits in reserve (as cash and other highly liquid assets). The borrowers sign an obligation to repay the loan plus interest or lose the house or car or whatever asset they have put as collateral. Then the loan is used to create more money, that is to back a new loan.

The system basically works like this: Say 10'000US$ is deposited in a bank. The bank can then give a loan of 10'000US$ minus the fraction reserve requirement. Say the fraction is 10%, then the loan the bank can give is 9'000US$. This loan is used to pay for something. Now, if this money that the seller get is put in a bank (the same or another) it can be used for this bank for another loan. That is, it can be used as a basis of a new loan of 9'000US$ minus the fraction reserve requirement. That is 9'000US$ - 900US$ = 8'100US$. Table 1 shows how this will continue.

Table 1 Fractional reserve system example. Starting with 10'000US$.

Loan no	Loan amount	Total lent out
1	9'000US$	9'000US$
2	8'100US$	17'100US$
3	7'300US$	24'400US$
4	6'600US$	31'000US$
5	5'900US$	36'900US$
.	.	.
.	.	.

The table shows an example where some money got from a central bank is used to produce commercial bank money via successive re-lending and where we use a reserve rate of 10% [22].

This means however that banks do not have enough money to pay out if too many want to withdraw their money at the same time, a phenomenon called a **bank run**. One way to prevent bank runs is to have a way of supplying more money when needed. This is called "elastic currency" and it is one of the functions of the Federal Reserve System [23] to supply this. This has indeed resulted in more money and even more money and more money - leading to inflation:

- $122.76 in the year 1913 had the same "purchase power" as $100 in the year 1774.

---

[22] The actual reserve rate varies. At http://en.wikipedia.org/wiki/Money_creation you can find an example (which uses a reserve rate of 20%) that is much more complete than our example.

[23] The Federal Reserve system (sometimes just called the Federal Reserve or Fed) was created in 1913 with the passing of the Federal Reserve Act.

It supervises and regulates banking institutions to ensure safety, soundness and stability of the nation's banking and financial system.

It's main task is to solve the problem inherent with fractional-reserve banking; namely, bank runs.

- $2242.74 in the year 2008 had the same "purchase power" as $100 in the year 1913.[24]

That is, 23% inflation in the 139 years between 1774 and 1913 but 2243% inflation in the 95 years between 1913 and 2008. The Federal Reserve System was created in 1913. Now I wonder, could there be a connection here somewhere? Hmm . . .

This way for banks to increase the sum of money is thus one way to create "extra" bubble money and it makes it possible for market prices to run away to new highs. If the total sum of money was limited in some reasonable way to the sum total of real value in a society this would not be possible.

This is exactly where the idea of barter money comes in. Of course it is not possible to determine the sum total of barter money exactly down to the last digit but to keep letting a very bad idea, the market function alone, set prices because we do not have a perfect replacement is of course exceedingly foolish, close to madness.

To begin with we should let the idea that money is indeed sterile as already Aristotle understood sink into our worldview. If we could truly understand this we could turn away from inventing new money schemes and instead turn our eyes to creating real value, true wealth. And when we have got more trealth we can adjust the amount of barter money to reflect this. We would then by the way avoid inflation!

Thus, only when we create real value should we allow the money supply to expand. That is, when we increase the sum of commodities and/or services. The formulas used also hints at how this can be done, by changing one or both of the arguments H and T. If we can make people work 10% more time the sums ought to go up 10%. Unless people get sick because they work too much in which case the sum of produced commodities and/or services might actually drop.

The sum of commodities may also not go up 10% because we may run into a shortage of materials used to make these commodities

---

[24] I have used http://www.measuringworth.com/ppowerus/result.php for these figures.

for instance. Thus increasing the *H* input is a very uncertain way of increasing trealth.

What is left is varying the *T* input. We can increase the level of available ideas – use better technology. Simply put, to focus on finding and encouraging new good ideas to emerge and be used to create new products and services. That is the way we have travelled for thousands of years and in particular during the last couple of hundreds of years in a quite successful way. In fact between 1870 and 1990 the productivity increased with more than 3'000% in Japan, more than 2'000% in Sweden and about 1'200% in USA.[25] So that should of course be the way we should continue to go. So how do we make production go up? Economists talk about something called factors of production so that will be the subject for our next chapter.

Summary

We started by noting that technology, in short, can be said to be the sum of the ways in which social groups provides themselves with the material objects and other nice things of their civilization. The nice things we want we call trealth and our basic equation for this was:

$$trealth = \sum_{all,wanted} commodity_i + \sum_{all,wanted} service_i$$

We also noted that the total sum of money that can be used in a society, that is:

$$\sum_{all} money = \sum_{a,w} b(commodity_i) + \sum_{a,w} b(service_i)$$
$$+ \sum_{all} bubble\ money$$

can be increased in two different ways:

1. By creating new and better commodities and services or,

---

[25] August Maddison, 1982, OECD 1991.

2. by getting involved in different economic schemes which produce different types of bubble money.

We looked a little closer at one popular way for banks to create more bubble money called the fractional reserve system.

In this chapter we also stated the view that trealth is highly dependent on the level of technology. Increasing true wealth can only be done if the level of technology is increased which is the same as saying that only new and better ideas can give us more real wealth, what we call trealth in this book.

Factors of Production

> *All intelligent thoughts have already been thought; what is necessary is only to try to think them again. [Johann Wolfgang von Goethe]*

How can we get out of this mess of speculation and rampant economic bubbles? The first step is to understand that we must get back to building trealth instead of wealth. Let's look at our equations.

$$trealth = f(H,T), \qquad \frac{\partial f(H,T)}{\partial t} > 0$$

$$trealth = c(H,T) + s(H,T) = \sum_{a,w} commodity_i + \sum_{a,w} service_i$$

The first equation simply expresses the view that trealth depends on H and T and that increasing technology will increase trealth. Normally the more we work or the better technology we have the more trealth can be produced. But as was pointed out earlier the dependency on H is more obscure since increasing the amount of worked hours is difficult, especially if people get sick because they have to work too much. And since trealth is what we want and many people actually want to work less and spend more time with their children, to write that book or perhaps even start up that company of their own, working more hours in the traditional sense – as an employee – to increase trealth soon becomes a contradiction. That is, if trealth is to work less but we have to work more to get more trealth we have a paradox.

So let's look more at the T input, technology. What does the current level of technology and future possible technology depend on? This question can be expressed this way:

$$T = t(parameter\ 1, parameter\ 2\ .....)$$

Where t is the function that determines the T argument in the $trealth = f(H, T)$ equation. Which are the inputs that produce an effect, preferably an increase in T? I can think of several: The educational level of people, the amount of available information and the ease of access to information, available tools and technology itself.

But let's start by taking a look at what the economists says. They talk about factors of production which sounds promising. Factors of production are various types of resources used in the production of goods and services. **Goods** are tangible material items that can be consumed now or later, and **services** are intangible tasks that are consumed at the same time as they are produced (like hair styling). Sounds a lot like our commodities and services does it not? It is of course the same, at least in principle.

If we want an equation for this – and we do want that! – we can write it like this:

$$Production\ of\ goods\ and\ services\ in\ a\ country$$
$$= p(factors\ of\ production)$$

That is, the production in a country is a function (here called p) of the *factors of production*. Now we want to write things short so we prefer the following:

$$P = p(factors\ of\ production)$$

Sir William Petty (1623-87) first defined **land** and **labor** as factors of production. Capital was soon added as another production factor and lately also "entrepreneurship and management" skills has been added and is regarded by many as a production factor too. There are also other factors such as human capital [26] but the first four (land, labor, capital, entrepreneurship /management skills) are the major ones.

Surprisingly capital is in this context not quite what we are used to think it is. That is, if we look up capital in a dictionary, we may often read that capital is wealth, as in money or property. But when

---

[26] Human capital refers to the available skills and knowledge found in the workers.

considered as a production factor **capital** is the things that we have constructed to be used to produce things (that is what makes it a production factor!) Perhaps there is hope for some of the economists?

Capital is thus the buildings, machinery, tools (often called fixed capital) or the stock of goods (such as raw materials, that are used to produce final products often called circulating capital) which are used for producing goods and services. Sometimes you can see the concept **capital goods** to denote human made goods or means of production to distinguish it from the more general term capital.

Capital is the only factor which itself is created in the production process. To indicate that our capital is not money we denote it with C_{tmg} (tools, machinery and intermediate goods).

Thus we can refine our equation above considering only the four major production factors:

$$P = p(L_n, L_b, C_{tmg}, E_m)$$

L_n stands for the production factor land and L_b stands for the production factor labor. E_m stands for **entrepreneurship** and good management skills.

The returns or payments for each of these factors are rent for land, wage for labor, interest for capital, and profit for entrepreneurship.

Capital and labor are regarded as active factors while land is passive. One can only shift capital and labor rather than land which is given limited.

Leaving this Stone Age way of viewing things we consider how these factors are related to the level of technology.

Land, L_n

Land, L_n are natural resources used in the creation of products such as geographical locations, mineral deposits like coal and iron ore and so on. These things are by economists considered to be fixed.

However, is land really fixed? In one sense, yes but in another sense not at all. Land in the sense of (land) area on the surface of the earth is a bit difficult to increase but they have added some land area in the Netherland due to an existing technology to do so. We could also get more usable land if the technology to water deserts was improved.

But land also includes natural resources such as iron ore. Take bog iron ore for instance. Bog iron ore is the impure iron deposits that develop in bogs, swamps and some lakes. This was once an important source of iron. However, this source of iron was not available during the Stone Age due to a lack of technology for converting it to iron. They just did not have any iron during the Stone Age. They probably did not even know what it was. Think about that!

Today we have the technology for making iron from bog iron ore but we do not do that. Why? Because we have other better technology that makes it possible to get more iron and of better quality from other sources. Thus we see that the input L_n (for land) depends on the level of technology (as well as on how many hours that has been worked).

We can also take the example with iron ore a step further. During for instance the 16th century most of the iron ore we dig up today in modern mines was as inaccessible as iron ore on the moon is to us today. Why was it inaccessible? The answer is lack of technology.

This leads to a fascinating question: Will iron ore (or another ore) on the moon always be inaccessible to us – in the sense that it will not be mined? That is a question of technology too is it not? Thus land for all *practical* considerations is not fixed at all. Especially if we consider space, the availability of which is definitely directly dependent on the level of technology! Thus L_n depends heavily on the level of available technology. We sum up these arguments like this:

$$L_n = l(H,T), \qquad \frac{\partial l(H,T)}{\partial h} > 0, \qquad \frac{\partial l(H,T)}{\partial t} > 0$$

Labor, L_b

Labor, L_b is the human effort, whether manual or mental provided in the creation of products and services and that is added to the production process. What does this depend on? Well, how many hours we work of course but also on the educational level and available information and how easy it is to access information for instance. Let's stop there, we have enough factors to get ahead. The equation for the educational level:

$$E_d = e(H,T), \qquad \frac{\partial e(H,T)}{\partial h} > 0, \qquad \frac{\partial e(H,T)}{\partial t} > 0$$

This equation says that the more time (H) we spend on getting educated and the better the supporting technology (T) is for this the more educated (E_d) we get. That sounds reasonable does it not. Why else would we have schools?

In the same way, the more time (H) we spend on accumulating knowledge and systematizing it and the better the supporting technology (T) is for this the more information (I) we ought to get. We formulate this argument like this:

$$I = i(H,T), \qquad \frac{\partial i(H,T)}{\partial h} > 0, \qquad \frac{\partial i(H,T)}{\partial t} > 0$$

Using these equations in an equation for labor we get:

$$L_b = g(E_d, I, H) = g(e(H,T), i(H,T), H)$$

That is L_b is a function g[27] of E_d, I and H. Actually this description of how things depend on each other can be reduced to (with some information loss):

$$L_b = g(H,T)$$

Because it is equally true that the better educated we are and the more information we have access to and can use intelligently the better we will work. We sum up these arguments like this:

---

[27] We use g instead of l or b because l is already used for land and b is used for the barter function.

$$L_b = g(H,T), \qquad \frac{\partial g(H,T)}{\partial h} > 0, \qquad \frac{\partial g(H,T)}{\partial t} > 0$$

Capital, C_{tmg}

Remembering that capital (C_{tmg}) stands for tools, machinery and goods that can be used to produce things C_{tmg} we get the equation:

$$C_{tmg} = tmg(H,T)$$

Because it is very hard to deny that the tools, the machinery and the intermediate products used in production today do depend directly on available technology. The very reason that we today have the tools that we have is a direct result of new ideas that make up our present technology. If any economists try to say anything else just shut him or her up. You have my permission to do so. Thus we also get this strong argument:

$$C_{tmg} = tmg(H,T), \qquad \frac{\partial tmg(H,T)}{\partial t} > 0$$

Entrepreneurship & Management, E_m

Since we defined technology as the sum of new ideas including ideas for management it is quite clear that this factor also depends in a positive factor on technology. And since this factor also ought to depend on how much time we spend on following up things, checking that we are on track and spending time making sure people are motivated and so on we get a positive dependency also on the time we spend on this. Thus:

$$E_m = m(H,T), \qquad \frac{\partial m(H,T)}{\partial h} > 0, \qquad \frac{\partial m(H,T)}{\partial t} > 0$$

Dependency on Technology

Let's return to our equation above:

$$P = p(L_n, L_b, C_{tmg}, E_m)$$

And insert our new equations into it:

$$P = p\big(l(H,T), g(H,T), tmg(H,T), m(H,T)\big)$$

This formula expresses the view that the production of goods and services in a country is a function of land, labor, tools-machinery-goods and entrepreneurship & management skills. Or stated more mathematically: The production P in a country is a function p of the functions l, g, *tmg* and m. And these functions (l, g, *tmg* and m) are a function of the inputs T and H.

Now since the factors of production are considered to be resources used in the production we must assume the obvious, the more of these factors the more production we get. Adding to this the arguments (summarized with our equations) that these production factors depend heavily on technology and that increasing technology will increase these factors we have again a strong argument indeed for asserting that increasing technology will have a deep and positive impact on production.

Thus we can again state the obvious: The key to increasing production is new and better ideas.

The reason for stating the obvious is of course that this obvious fact does not seem to influence economists much. They spend all their time on balancing the budget. Firing people to boost the price of shares and indulge in very inventive ideas to "make money" of which we mentioned a few in our earlier chapter *In the Beginning*. For instance "hedging," "speculation and arbitrage," "OTC and exchange traded," "bilateral netting," "gross negative fair value," "notional amount," "perpetual preferred shareholders equity."

And if we steal the trick from the economists to use mathematics to be more impressive we can state the obvious this way:

$$P = p\big(l(H,T), g(H,T), tmg(H,T), m(H,T)\big), \qquad \frac{\partial p(H,T)}{\partial t} > 0$$

Then it ought to become more difficult to deny the dominating factor of T, that is new ideas, as the most important argument for building trealth.

Summary

We looked at the factors of production and saw that it was quite easy to argue that they depend on the level of technology. The higher level of technology we have, the more production we get. We found strong arguments indeed for asserting that increasing technology will have a deep and positive impact on production.

Thus we can again state the obvious: The keys to increasing production are new and better ideas.

The reason for stating the obvious is of course that this obvious fact does not seem to influence economists much. They just keep on talking about money, inflation, balanced budgets and so on while the whole world shakes and money-bubbles burst.

Source and Support Processes

A cynic is a man who knows the price of everything but the value of nothing. [Oscar Wilde]

Where does trealth come from? When we try to untangle the mystery of where it all begins we soon find that the it is all very interrelated in obscure ways due to our complex society.

To get some insight, let's simplify and take a rather typical case where some small industrial community loses its main dominant company. What happens then is that everything slows down when the workers have to go and live on unemployment compensations. Reduced income results in fewer purchases in stores and less tax being paid. Stores and the municipality may have to dismiss people. People without jobs may have to move away from the community to get work somewhere else and this in its turn leads to even less commercial revenue and internal revenue in a negative progression of events until some new equilibrium is reached at a (much) lower level of activity. This example indicates that we have at least three manners of functioning or operating; we have three different processes, systematic series of actions directed to some end:

- **Source processes**. A company such as the one described above is in some way the start or the beginning of all activities in the industrial community. It can be viewed as a source of trealth production.
- **Private supporting processes**. These support both the employees with restaurants, stores and so on but also the source processes themselves through subcontractors and other business that service the source processes. Examples of this include supplying needed services such as repairing machines, booking air and train tickets, bookkeeping, office supplies, transports and so on. All these "secondary" private processes are thus supporting the source processes either directly or indirectly.

- **Public supporting processes**. These are the public services. These too support the employees and the source processes by delivering health care, electricity, fire service, police service and so on. Important services that are needed to make the source processes run smoothly.

The basic difference between a source process and a support process is the dependency. If we apply a flow perspective, the source processes provide a determining start for the life in a community much like plankton do for aquatic life. No plankton, no source of food for life in the seas and no source process not much life in a community.

Support processes thus have a fundamental dependency on the existence of source processes. Source processes also depend on support processes but this is more a question of efficiency than of sheer survival. Take away a service that help the source process by booking airline tickets or a service that supply electricity and the source process will survive *because a source process can replace missing external support processes with internal support processes*. Let someone employed at the company book the tickets, a company can build a power plant of their own if they cannot get electricity any other way and so on. This actually often happens when a company comes to a development country and finds that supporting processes are not available or are of so low quality that they cannot rely on them.

The opposite is not true. The ticket booking service cannot survive without the company.

Of course this description is a model and as such it is connected to a certain purpose, namely to show how different types of companies depend on each other. It could for instance be argued that our company is no more a source process than an agency that helps customer book tickets because our company is also dependent on customers. But why then is it that the whole community slows down when that big dominating company shuts down but that not much happens if a ticket agency shuts down in that community? So there is a true insight gained with this example that in some way there is indeed a start of trealth production. This "start" is harder to see clearly today than it was a long time ago when farms – and in some places fisheries – were the most common source processes but the dependency on source processes is still there and it is important that we can see it.

Private and Public Services

Public services are of course things we want so they are true wealth, trealth. We can break public services out of our trealth equation and we then get:

$$trealth = \sum_{a,w} commodity_i + \sum_{a,w} private\ service_i + \sum_{a,w} public\ service_i$$

I guess it is true that public services may also produce an occasional commodity but let's leave that and use the above formula.

In many ways the sum of public services represent trealth to a greater extent than the sum of private services. This is because they are so essential to us that for moral reasons they must be guaranteed whereas we could survive without many of the private services that are offered on the market. It could be argued that many of the private services – especially those concerned with advertising - are not contributing any real wealth at all, they are just there to make us buy more, eat more or even smoke more.

If you are an economist you would probably prefer a perspective where we talked about **value added** instead. That is, the additional value of a commodity over the cost of commodities used to produce it from a previous stage of production. In short, the contribution of the factors of production, to raising the value of a product. If we did that our ticket booking service would also contribute "value added" as our company and the dependencies we try to illustrate would become much more obscure. We would of course also immediately be returned to a price/money perspective since the "value added" concept is connected to money (price, cost per unit) and that is definitely something that this book tries to avoid!

It should by now be clear how the ideas/concepts we have accepted steer us along a certain path of thinking. To go another path we need other ideas. As we said in one of the first chapters *Everything Begins with Ideas*.

Let us return to the source and support process perspective. We can then talk about a **fundamental dependency** between the support processes and the source process and an **efficiency dependency** the other way. This is illustrated in Figure 2 where we illustrate this with an industrial community with one dominant source process, a company.

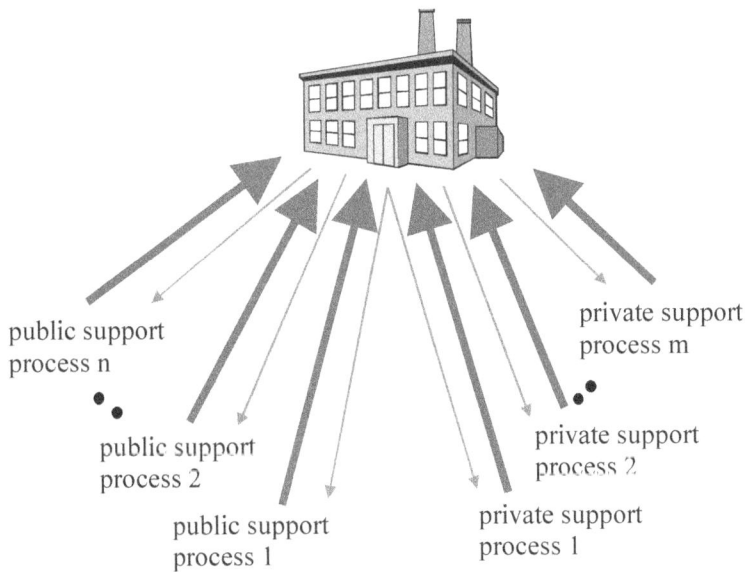

public support
process n

private support
process m

public support
process 2

private support
process 2

public support
process 1

private support
process 1

Figure 2 Fundamental dependencies (thick arrows) on a company and efficiency dependencies (thin arrows) the other way.

Fundamental dependencies are shown in Figure **2** with thick arrows and efficiency dependencies are shown with thin arrows. Let's redo our formula for trealth to reflect these ideas.

$$trealth = \sum_{a,w} source\ process_i + \sum_{a,w} private\ support\ process_i$$
$$+ \sum_{a,w} public\ support\ process_i$$

This little model express the view that the distinction between private companies and public service companies often made in discussions where private companies are put forward as the ones supporting us and where public services are seen as just a cost is a simplification that hides a very important fact: Not all private enterprises contribute "source." Both the private supporting processes and the public supporting processes depend on that source processes exist! The key to increase the amount of trealth is thus to make sure that we have an ample supply of source processes and that they can thrive because of available support processes. For example, thinking that *any* private enterprise will fix the situation for our industrial community example that lost its dominating industry is not very true. Only a *source* process will help!

There is thus no difference in how private support and public support processes depend on support processes. They both survive because of the source processes and if the source(s) goes away they will get the same type of problems. In this sense privatization is a rather meaningless fix for our industrial community example where the community lost its main source process because it would not fix the problem. We need more source processes – not just converting public support processes into private support processes!

The most important insight this little model suggests is thus that to help our industrial community we must have one or several new source processes! This conclusion is also applicable in a broader sense because it also applies to a large community or a whole country as such. It is just a bit more difficult to see the dependencies when more parties are involved than one single dominant industry.

Source Processes

Preferably a source process should produce a lot of "source" but what type of source process are we then talking about? Let's find an answer by asking ourselves some more questions. Why did the company in our example go out of business in the first place? The answer is simple, because it did not have competitive products of course. But why were the products not competitive?

Yes indeed, why are products not competitive? Let's ask ourselves even more questions. Why do we prefer a colour TV to a black and white TV? Why do we prefer an LCD screen to a CRT screen? Why do we prefer a modern car, a modern refrigerator or the latest mobile phone? It is either a question of lower price and/or better properties is it not? Better or new properties are directly related to new and better ideas – better technology – used in the product. However, price is also dependant on new ideas because new ideas can help make the production process more efficient and thereby reduce production costs resulting in less expensive products. Thus we are again returned to technology, T, as the key factor for creating trealth.

It is an increase in technology that can give us more desirable products and help us produce them at lower production costs. The focus should thus be on how this can come about. For instance, there is a need for a focus on raising the educational level of people.

What we need are thus not just new source processes but source processes with a high content of new ideas!

Of course an increase in tourism could also be a solution. Instead of a local flow of source from employees we then get a "long distance" flow of "source" from tourists when they do different things such as stay in hotels, eat at restaurants, pay for tourist excursions or just shop in the stores.

But these tourists are of course not source processes in themselves because their ability to start a flow of "source" depends on some other source process where they earned their "source." To distinguish between these sources we could say that the local source process is a **true source process** but that the tourists represent a **transferral source processes**.

Nota bene: The reason we want these source processes is not that they represent the most valuable trealth for us. Rather many of the public services such as high quality health services, education, police service, fire service and so on are the ones that represent trealth more than anything else for most of us. But, as discussed above, for these support processes to exist we do need source processes. That is, good high-tech companies that can give us desirable and usable commodities and services, pay taxes and employ people and give them high salaries.

When we speak about making the support processes better it is thus also because better support processes for our source processes will make them function more efficiently.

But we must not forget what it is that we really want. We should not be fooled into thinking that private enterprise and privatization is the single simple formula for increasing trealth. For example, companies that pay low salaries and that do not care for their employees do not represent any trealth at all and must be replaced by other companies or we will get a poor society.

Summary

The activities in a society can be viewed as being of two different types; There are source processes and support processes. A source process is in some way the start or the beginning of all activities in an industrial community. It can be viewed as a source of trealth production. What happens if such a source process goes away is that everything slows down in a society.

The basic difference between a source process and a support process is the dependency. If we apply a flow perspective, the source processes provide a determining start for the life in a community much like plankton do for aquatic life.

Preferably a source process should produce a lot of "source" and this is directly related to:

1. The amount of new ideas – technology – used in the service or product and,
2. the level of technology used in the production of it.

Support processes can be divided into private support processes and public support processes.

Both the private supporting processes and the public supporting processes depend on that source processes exist. The key to increase the amount of trealth is thus to make sure that we have an ample supply of source processes and that they can thrive because of available efficient support processes and the use of a high level of technology.

Scarce Resources?

Language is the dress of thought. [Samuel Johnson]

Limiting Resource

One way to look at systems is to view them as a way through which we allocate **scarce resources**. It is then often added that growth is limited by its most scarce resource(s) called **limiting resource**(s).

For example, in order to grow, a tree has to have water, sunlight, carbon dioxide and several trace minerals. If any of these resources is scarce enough that its absence keeps the tree from growing faster, then it is a limiting resource. Actually there can be several limiting resources in a system. If the paucity of a limiting resource is replaced by abundance then usually another resource becomes limiting.

The economy is then said to be similar to the tree example, in that it consumes resources and produces things. In chapter *Factors of Production* we had the following equation for production:

$$P = p(L_n, L_b, C_{tmg}, E_m)$$

Where:

L_n = land, natural resources.
L_b = labor, human effort.
C_{tmg} = capital, tools, machinery and intermediate goods.
E_m = entrepreneurship and good management.

Lack of natural resources, not enough workers and so on could all limit production. That is, any of these production factors could become a limiting resource.

However as we easily found out in chapter *Factors of Production*, all these production factors depend on technology in a positive way; An increase in technology can increase any and all of these production factors. That is, none of these production factors have to become scarce if we let technology develop enough. Or, using the concept of limiting resources we could say that the only true limiting resource is scarcity of new ideas.

This may come as a difficult to believe medicine for many. Since the concept of "raw materials" often surfaces up in connection with a discussion of scarcity let's select it for some discussion. Raw materials are part of the land factor function $l(H, T)$ closer described in chapter *Land*, L_n. There are many people that think that we can run out of raw materials. They say that we have a limited amount of raw materials implying that it can become a limiting resource. Now this is both very true but also very untrue.

Look at the case of bog iron ore mentioned earlier for instance. With the right technology we can skip bog iron and go for better mineral deposits deeper in the earth increasing the amount of iron available almost without limit. Well, if we go to the moon and go out into space the limit is very far away indeed.

However, this actually misses the most interesting aspects of new ideas – new technology. For instance when we say that we need some (raw) material it is namely nearly always *a question of realizing some objective for us.* For instance, we need oil to warm our house or gas to drive our car. ***With another technology we can use something else*** than oil to warm our house or something else than gas to make our car run. This is because it is actually ***not*** oil or gas that we need. We want a warm house and/or to be able to drive a car from A to B. In the latter case it may even be that we only want to get from A to B in a convenient way and that using a car is not a necessity. We summarize this argument with an equation where R stands for raw materials:

$$O = o(R, T, H)$$

The equation expresses the view that to realize objective O (a warm house, getting from A to B and so on) we need some process, represented by function o, that can realize this objective and input arguments are R (raw material), T (technology) and H (worked hours).

We could also have included E, energy, as an input but because energy is a function of technology and raw materials I see no need to include it as a special argument of its own.

R here denotes true raw materials such as iron ore, logs, and crude oil and cotton. However, we can of course also let R denote materials that have had some processing such as cotton refined into thread or even cloth or steel from iron ore or petrol. [28]

However, *it is seldom that we need some particular raw material*. Rather, we need to develop some capability that can realize our objective and we just happened to choose some particular raw material to implement this capability.

The Capability Equation

We introduce the capability equation:

$$C_p = capability(R, T) \; [util]$$

Inputs are R (raw material) and T (technology). This is simply a general idea to describe what the commodities and the services give us. That is, a commodity or a service or a combination of one or more of each are capable of delivering something to us that we want to have – a capability – such as warming a house or making a car move. We express the view that:

$$trealth = \sum_{all,wanted} capability_i(R, T)$$

Which says that the (sum of) trealth in a society is the sum of all (wanted) capabilities available, that is all the things we are able to do and get with available products and services in a society given available raw materials and available technology.

---

[28] This is not in exact accord with how raw materials are typically described in literature. Often raw materials to be called raw materials must only have undergone light processing. However, I let R also represent materials that has had more than light processing. Well, we live in a high-tech society do we not?

Since it takes time (worked hours) to get raw materials, develop technology and put all this together to create a capability, each capability has a cost in the form of worked hours. It is of course a bit complicated since, for instance, new technology can reduce the need of worked time to get some raw material. And, how many of the worked hours to create some technology shall we ascribe to some particular capability and so on?

We solve this by saying that we should always strive for the minimum amount of worked hours needed to develop a capability:

$$util\ value\ for\ a\ capability,\ C_p, in\ worked\ hours$$
$$= min(worked\ hours\ all\ available\ combinations\ of\ R\ and\ T\ in\ c(R,T))$$

Otherwise we could increase the util value by, for example wheat, by forbidding the reaping-machine and/or the combine-harvester.

Note also that it, is the capability we are after. Thus for instance an old radio using vacuum tubes would not increase in util value if vacuum tubes no longer were available and would have to be handmade which would take a lot of time thus increasing the time needed to (re)construct the radio. It is the capability of the radio we want and that can easily be replaced by a modern transistor radio thus the util value of the radio using vacuum tubes would ***not*** increase.

The above of course describes just one possible way to measure util.

We need Capabilities

The point we are making is that we need capabilities rather than some special raw material. For instance, in the car industry we may want to develop a shield put inside the doors so that if a car runs into the side of another car the passengers are protected from this impact.

Let's say that a first solution came up with a construction (using some technology T_1 and some raw material R_1) that resulted in a construction of steel that was then put in the door of the car. Further let's assume, better technology improved on this so that we could use less iron and still get the same capability to protect the passengers in an improved construction (using some technology T_2 and some raw material R_2). [29] Using the capability equation:

$$C_p = c(R, T)$$

We can describe this example in this way:

$$C_{p\,car\ door\ protection,1} = c(R_1, T_1)$$

$$C_{p\,car\ door\ protection,2} = c(R_2, T_2)$$

Where $R_2 < R_1$, but $T_2 > T_1$.

If the new construction has the same capability which we assume, we have been able to decrease the amount of needed raw materials by using new ideas, that is, increasing the level of technology. In fact it may even be possible that the new solution using less raw materials is even better. That is,

$$C_{p\,car\ door\ protection,2} > C_{p\,car\ door\ protection,1}$$

A well known example of greatly increasing the capability without increasing the use of raw material is the development of personal computers. Let $C_{p\,PC\ 1988}$, $C_{p\,PC\ 1998}$, $C_{p\,PC\ 2008}$ stand for the capability, that is, the processing power, functionality, diversity, usability and so on for a typical PC in 1988, 1998 and 2008 respectively.

$$C_{p\,PC\ 1988} = c(R_{PC\ 1988}, T_{PC\ 1988})$$

$$C_{p\,PC\ 1998} = c(R_{PC\ 1998}, T_{PC\ 1998})$$

---

[29] The example is taken from a fascinating exhibition called Ferrum at display at the National museum of science and technology in Stockholm.

$$C_{p_{PC\ 2008}} = c(R_{PC\ 2008}, T_{PC\ 2008})$$

Since personal computers are constructed from about the same amount of raw material it is true to state $R_{PC\ 1988} \approx R_{PC\ 1998} \approx R_{PC\ 2008}$.[30] In fact since at least stationary computers are so similar in use of raw material it is reasonable to say: $R_{PC\ 1988} = R_{PC\ 1998} = R_{PC\ 2008}$.

Now since $C_{p_{PC\ 1988}} \ll C_{p_{PC\ 1998}} \ll C_{p_{PC\ 2008}}$[31] the great increase in capability must depend on something else than R and using the equation $C_p = c(R, T)$ we see that this must be the T factor. The increase in capability is directly a consequence of an increase in T. In fact, it is of course true that $T_{PC\ 2008} \gg T_{PC\ 1998} \gg T_{PC\ 1988}$ and this explains the increase in capability. Thus, we again see an example where we are **not** dependant on more raw materials for increasing the functionality etc.

And R need not even have to be of the same type! For instance when telephone lines started to transfer more and more information it was once thought that we would run out of copper because we would need all these copper cables to transfer all the information that we started to transfer. But new technology such as digital transfer of data and the use of glass fibres instead of copper resulted in not only thinner cables but in a situation where we hardly need copper at all for this transfer of information. Thus a better equation for realizing an objective (O):

$$O = o(R, T, H)$$

such as a warm house, transfer of data or getting from A to B would be:

$$O = o(C_p, H)$$

---

[30] The symbol $\approx$ means approximately similar too.
[31] The symbol $\ll$ means much less than.

This equation describes our argumentation above better because we here focus less on raw materials and more on what is the true key to realizing an objective; an available capability to realize the objective (and some H (worked hours)).

In reality we would probably need several capabilities so a more complete equation would be this:

$$O = o\left(C_{p1}, C_{p2}, C_{p3}, \dots C_{pk}, H\right)$$

However, the equation with one capability input is enough to express our argumentation.

Thus talking about limited resources as if that is any problem is very misleading. Only if we set a fixed technological level and do not push ahead could we ever reach a point where we actually will run out of raw materials for realizing some objective. Simply because it is seldom the raw materials in isolation that we need. It is a capability we need, C_p, to realize som objective $o\left(C_p, H\right)$ we want to have. And since C_p can be implemented in many different ways using different possible selections of raw materials depending on the technology used, technology again surfaces as the key factor for us. That is, since there are several capabilities $C_{p_1} = c(R_1, T_1) = C_{p_2} = c(R_2, T_2) = C_{p_3} = c(R_3, T_3), \dots$ that can perform the same thing we need not be restricted to some particular raw material R_1 in order to achieve some objective. The capabilities act like substitutes that can replace each other.

Talking about scarce resources and limiting resources is thus very misleading. It is not that the idea is always wrong. It certainly is true for the tree example! No, the problem is analogous to the problem with the demand and supply scenario often used by economists. This scenario makes us think about money and price instead of increasing trealth through new ideas.

The idea of limiting resources also locks us into a certain mind-set where we focus on the wrong things. Instead of searching for ways to expand and improve enabling technologies we may think that raw materials or the amount of hours we can work are limiting us. But that does not matter because if these things are limited, through the application of new technology these limitations can be overcome as they have repeatedly been overcome in the past.

Only in a few special cases such as for jewellery where someone may insist on using gold is there a need for a particular type of raw material.

However, setting a fixed technological level would be a sure ticket to problems and poverty because then we would not have a replacing capability but would keep on consuming the raw materials needed for some particular capability.

For instance, if we need a certain capability for some task, $C_{p_1} = c(R_1, T_1)$, and we keep on using that we may find that we do not someday have enough raw material, R_1, and we cannot use any of the possible alternates $C_{p_2} = c(R_2, T_2)$ or $C_{p_3} = c(R_3, T_3)$ since none of the possible technologies T_2 or T_3 are available (if we have set a fixed technological level).

Summary

We expressed the view that trealth could be measured by the more general idea; by summing capabilities - what the commodities and the services give us.

$$trealth = \sum_{all,wanted} c_i(R, T)$$

To extract iron from bog iron we needed new ideas – new technology. However even better technology has helped us to extract much more iron in more efficient ways. Technology can thus increase the amount of available resources.

However, the most interesting aspects of technology is that with new technology we can find substitutes and use something else because it is seldom that we need some particular raw material. Rather, we need some capability – rather than some raw material - to realize some objective such as transferring information or warming a house. New technology has made it possible to heat a house with electricity from nuclear power plants and it has replaced copper cables using old technology with new technology to transfer data using glass fibres.

Talking about scarce resources and limiting resources is thus very misleading. It locks us into a certain mind-set where we focus on the wrong things. Instead of searching for ways to expand and improve enabling technologies – new ideas – we may think that raw materials or the amount of hours we can work are limiting us – but that is not the point. It does not matter if these things are limited, through new technology these limitations can be overcome as they have repeatedly been overcome in the past.

Only if we fix a technological level and do not push ahead could we ever reach a point where we actually will run out of raw materials for realizing some objective. This is so because then we would not have any replacing capability but would keep on consuming the raw materials needed for some particular capability.

Demand and Supply

Our ideas are only intellectual instruments which we use to break into phenomena; we must change them when they have served their purpose, as we change a blunt lancet that we have used long enough. [Claude Bernard]

The Model

The model of demand and supply is probably the most widely used model in economics. So what does it tell us? It says two things:

1. If the price goes up consumers will buy less (and vice versa) as shown in Figure 3. [32]
2. If the prices goes up producers will produce more (and vice versa) as shown in Figure 4.

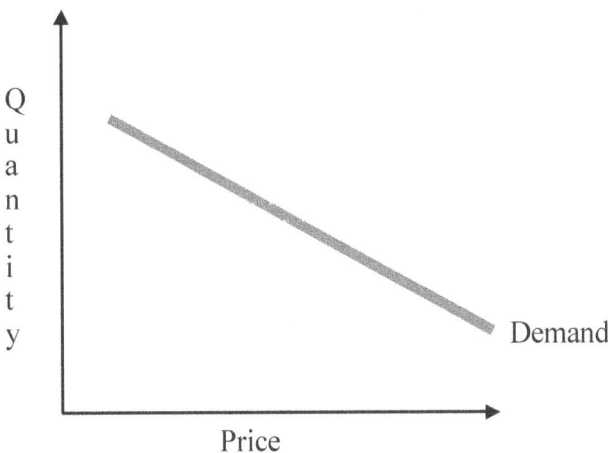

Figure 3 Consumers tend to buy less when price goes up.

---

[32] The curves are often shown not as straight lines as here but as slightly convex or concav curves. That does not change the conclusions drawn here though.

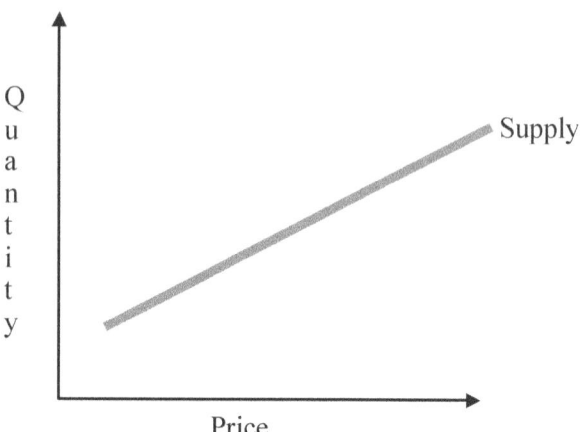

Figure 4 Producers tend to produce more when price goes up.

To make it a bit more interesting economists use to put these two revelations together to find that there appears to be a price where the consumers want to buy as much as the producers want to produce, the equilibrium price shown in Figure 5. This figure by the way show one of the benefits of talking "mathematics" - how easy it is to combine different ideas.

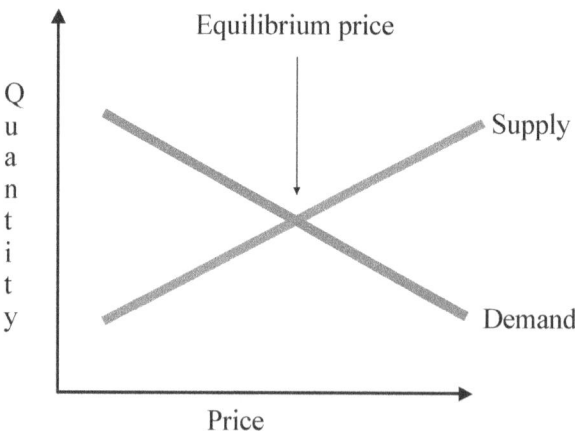

Figure 5 At the equilibrium price we consume all that is produced, no more no less. (Says the economists.)

Figure 5 with variations is a typical way of showing how a market price is set. The argumentation usually goes something like this:

- The higher the price, the more (supply) of a product or service will be available because companies will be more and more interested in supplying a product or service the higher the price is.
- On the other hand, the higher the price is, the less inclined to buy will the customers be so the demand will go down when the price goes up.
- At some point – the equilibrium price – the demand and supply curves will meet and the market will produce just as much as the companies will want to manufacture. No waste and everybody can be happy.

There is a lot more that can be said and unfortunately is said in schools and other places about these ideas. For instance economists use to show that if the price is not at the equilibrium price forces will be set in action that will change the demand and supply curves so that we again arrive at an equilibrium point.

Let's take an example, wheat, to illustrate this. In Table 2 I have put together some estimates using figures found on the internet. Exact prices and the quantities are not necessary since we only want to illustrate the principles so here goes:

Table 2 Wheat demanded at different prices. (USA)

P (Farm price per bushel)	Q_d (Quantity of wheat demanded per year (millions of bushels) at the given price)
$6	1'800
$8	1'600
$10	1'400

Of course a table for how much bushels the producers want to produce can also be manufactured and is shown in Table 3.

Table 3 Wheat supplied (produced) at different prices. (USA)

P (Farm price per bushel)	Q_s (Quantity of wheat supplied per year (millions of bushels) at the given price)
$6	1'400
$8	1'800
$10	2'300

If we plot these values in a figure we get Figure 6.

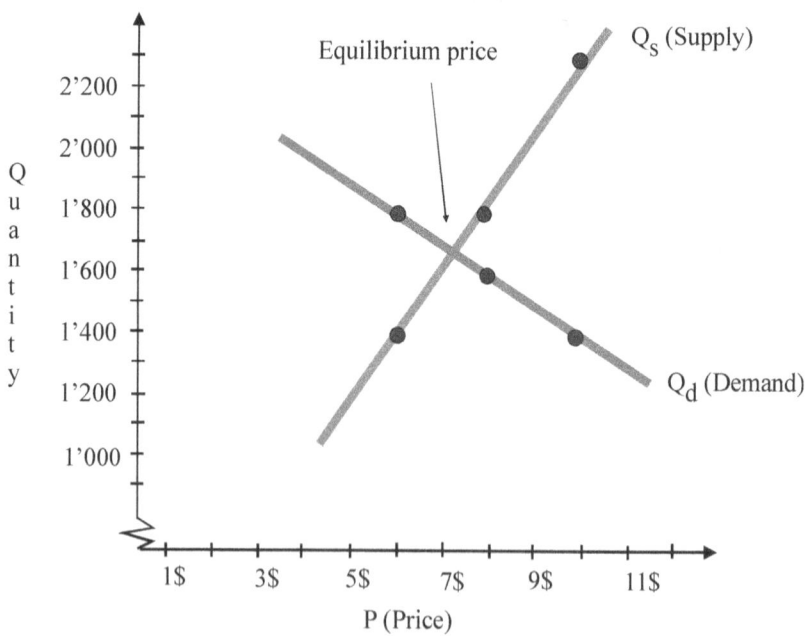

Figure 6 A possible equilibrium price for wheat.

In this figure we have three black dots for each curve that represent the entries in our two tables Table 2 and Table 3.

The line going down, demand line Q_d in Figure 6, shows that the quantity of wheat demanded decreases as the price rises. This is often referred to as the **law of demand**, which states that other things being equal, the higher the price of a good, the smaller is the quantity demanded.

And vice versa, if the price goes down consumers will buy more wheat, and less of other commodities that are substitutes for wheat such as corn. The same, if the price of wheat goes up, many people will start to eat more of rice, potatoes and/or sweet corn instead. These alternatives are thus called **substitutes**.

Figure 6 shows that the demand for something Q_d decreases with increasing price. In mathematical notation, we can describe this behaviour like this: [33]

$$Q_d = f_a(P), \qquad f_a'(P) < 0$$

Economists agree that price is not the only factor that influences how much we buy so the function $Q_d = f_a(P)$ is a simplification. The function should more properly be written:

$$Q_d = f_a\big(P, P_{pref}, E_{expectations}, \qquad \dots \big)$$

Where P_{pref} stands for personal preferences, $E_{expectations}$ stands for expectations of future prices and ... stands for all other inputs that can change Q_d.

There is also a **law of supply**: other things equal, the higher the price of a good – here wheat – the greater is the quantity supplied. This is shown by the line Q_s going up in Figure 6 and is also just common sense. If producers are paid more they tend to start producing more. Using mathematical notation to describe this we get: [34]

---

[33] This $f'(P) < 0$ is a derivative. If the derivative is negative it means that the function is decreasing with increasing P.

[34] $f'(P) > 0$ is mathematical notation that says that the derivative is positive which means that the function is increasing with increasing P.

$$Q_s = f_s(P), \quad f_s'(P) > 0$$

Happily enough when reading about this we can see that economists understand that there are more factors than price that influence this function too. This includes costs of factors of production, prices of related products, expected future prices and even technology. A better function description should thus be something like this:

$$Q_s = f_s\left(P, F_{production}, P_{related\ products}, E_{exp\ prices}, T, ...\right)$$

The inputs should be obvious. However, economists tend to stick to the simple case where the quantity only depends on one input (P). As we by now know, economists love to talk about money (price) as the major factor in life.

It is common to use straight lines to simplify the mathematics as we have done in our figures. Straight lines follow the familiar equation [35] $y = kx + l$ and we then get:

$$Q_d = k_d P + l_d, \qquad k_d < 0$$

$$Q_s = k_s P + l_s, \qquad k_s > 0$$

Q_d decreases with price, thus $k_d < 0$.

Q_s increases with price, thus $k_s > 0$.

Fitting a straight line to given samples (the black dots in Figure 6) can be done with for instance the method of least squares. Nothing so fancy here though, we just make a quick approximation directly from the graphs and get:

$$Q_d = -100P + 2'400$$

---

[35] Mathematicans prefer to write things short, thus they leave out the multiplication sign that is implied between k and x in $y = kx + l$.

$Q_s = 180P + 400$

Inputting our values (black dots) we get two tables. Table 4 shows that our first approximation is an exact fit using our equations whereas the equation used in Table 5 is a not quite so good fit.

Table 4 Comparing real demand and demand using an equation.

P	Q_d	$Q_d = -100P + 2'400$
$6	1'800	1'800
$8	1'600	1'600
$10	1'400	1'400

Table 5 Comparing real supply and supply using an equation.

P	Q_s	$Q_s = 180P + 400$
$6	1'400	1'480
$8	1'800	1'840
$10	2'300	2'200

Using the two equations:

$Q_d = -100P + 2'400$

$Q_s = 180P + 400$

We can calculate the equilibrium price because that is when demand meets supply, or $Q_d = Q_s$. That is, in this case:

$$-100P + 2'400 = 180P + 400$$

Just putting the P:s on the same side and the numbers on the other side we get:

$$2'400 - 400 = 180P + 100P$$

$$2'000 = 280P$$

$$P \approx 7$$

This corresponds nicely with Figure 6.

If we deviate from this price, the reasoning goes, at a price of $10 per bushel, there would be 1'400 million bushels demanded but there would be 2'300 million bushels supplied and we would have an excess supply (surplus) of 900 million bushels per year.

To get rid of unwanted inventories, producers would have to begin to offer their wheat at lower prices. There will be a downward pressure on the price.

The opposite can of course also occur, if the price of wheat were $6 per bushel, the supply would be only 1'400 million bushels but the demand would be 1'800 million bushels. This would encourage producers to raise prices which would lead to more being produced and we would again see a process towards the equilibrium price.

Such is the idea. That is, that in the actual market, price will move to the equilibrium price in a competitive market. However, in markets with price ceilings (as with rent control) or price floors (as with the minimum wage) we will have a price that is not equal to the equilibrium, and this will then lead to either a shortage or a surplus. This is then seen as obviously very wrong and bad.

The major problems with these simple models are that they are Cialdini shortcuts. There are so many other aspects that influences how people buy things that they can easily make the idea of the equilibrium price fallacious. For instance, the simple relation shown in Figure 3 can be just the opposite! There is namely a well-known stereotype that says "expensive = good." The most classic case of this is perhaps what happened with "Chivas Regal Scotch Whisky which had been a struggling brand until its managers decided to raise its price to a level far above its competitors. Sales skyrocketed, even though nothing was changed in the product itself." [36]

Not only is the way of reasoning shown above a simplification – a typical Cialdini shortcut – but there are several additional cardinal faults:

1. The model disregards the morals of the situation. Yes, the market may reach an equilibrium price where as much dental care is produced that can be paid for by the members of a society. But surely, there will still be a real shortage of dental care because not all that need it will get it! Only as much as the members are able to pay for will be produced. What type of nice equilibrium is that? Thus, this argument that at the equilibrium level there is no waste proposed as an objective neutral "fact," taught in schools and dominating the thoughts of most every economist is in reality a very political and biased argument. It is not an objective argument at all.

2. The second cardinal fault is the one we hinted at above, Q_d and Q_s are not only dependant on P. There are other factors than price that are of enormous importance which while often briefly mentioned for all practical purposes are ignored.

3. The model may work fairly well for some products and services, less well for other products and services and perhaps not at all for other products and services.

We will start by looking at fault number 2 by adding two other factors, advertisement and technology, respectively. And, we will do this using the tools the economists use to illustrate the problems to make our argumentation strong.

Lastly we will take a look at cardinal fault number 3.

---

[36] Influence, science and practice, Robert B. Cialdini Ph.D., page 6.

Advertising

It was pointed out above that $Q_d = f_d(P)$ is a simplification. Let's introduce advertising A as a factor [37]:

$$Q_{d,a} = f_d(P, A)$$

How will advertising change this? Advertising if it is any good will of course increase demand! That is, if it shall be reasonable to use advertising we must assume:

$$\frac{\partial f_d(P, A)}{\partial a} > 0$$

And given the same price:

$$Q_{d,a} > Q_d$$

We had the $Q_d = k_d P + l_d$ equation for Q_d. So we can write this equation for $Q_{d,a}$:

$$Q_{d,a} = k_{d,a} P + l_{d,a}$$

And using $Q_{d,a} > Q_d$ we get:

$$k_{d,a} P + l_{d,a} > k_d P + l_d$$

To simplify this we take two cases, $l_{d,a} = l_d$ and $k_{d,a} = k_d$. The first case is shown in Figure 7. Because $l_{d,a} = l_d$ we get:

$$k_{d,a} P + l_{d,a} > k_d P + l_{d,a}$$

Simplifying this by removing $l_{d,a}$ and dividing with P we get:

$$k_{d,a} > k_d$$

---

[37] The interested reader is also referred to "Appendix, More about Functions."

This just means that as price goes up, demand decreases less with price increases when advertising is used. This is in correspondence with what we assumed. We have simply converted what we assumed into the language of mathematics so that we can draw our lines.

Figure 7 shows that the new equilibrium price is higher. The customer is willing to pay more. ($P_{d,a} > P_d$).

We can express that like this:

$$P_{d,a} = P_d + C_{d,a} + P_{p+}, \qquad C_{d,a} > 0, \qquad P_{p+} > 0$$

The price paid, $P_{d,a}$, is equal to the price paid without advertising (P_d) plus the cost for advertising ($C_{d,a}$) plus extra profit for the producer (P_{p+}). As earlier stated, we assume that the marketing is successful! If profit does not go up with advertising why should a capitalist advertise his or her product(s)?

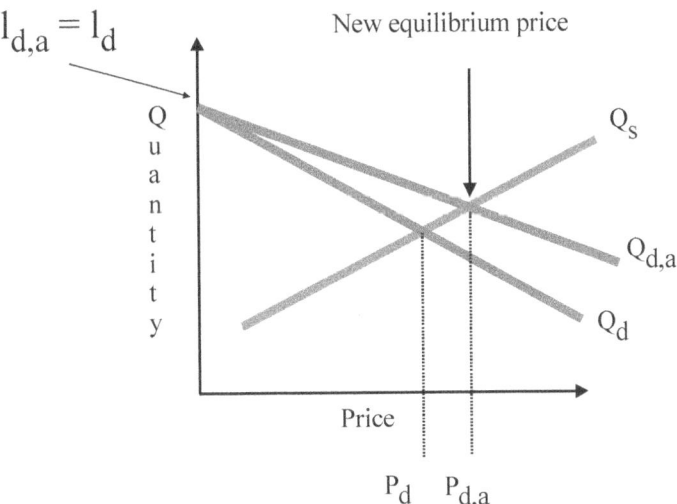

Figure 7 Advertising makes the price go up.

Or, in other words, the customer gets exactly the same product but has to pay more for it. Yes, I have heard the argument that advertising

increase sales so much that the production costs goes down, let's say
it goes down with an amount L_{prod}. Thus the advertising cost is
compensated by a lower production costs and in this case:

$$P_{d,a} = P_d + C_{d,a} + P_{p+} - L_{prod}$$

And L_{prod} is so high that we will get:

$$P_{d,a} < P_d$$

Well, branded goods are a typical good that is advertised a lot. How
many cases have you heard of where a branded good costs less than
its equivalent none-branded good? Ha! So much for that argument!
No, the flash and glitter added by heavy advertising just increases the
price but does not contribute any more trealth. Of course, wheat may
not be the best example to illustrate the pitfalls with advertising.

The other case $k_{d,a} = k_d$ results in this equation:

$$k_{d,a}P + l_{d,a} > k_{d,a}P + l_d$$

Simplifying we get:

$$l_{d,a} > l_d$$

This is shown in Figure 8.

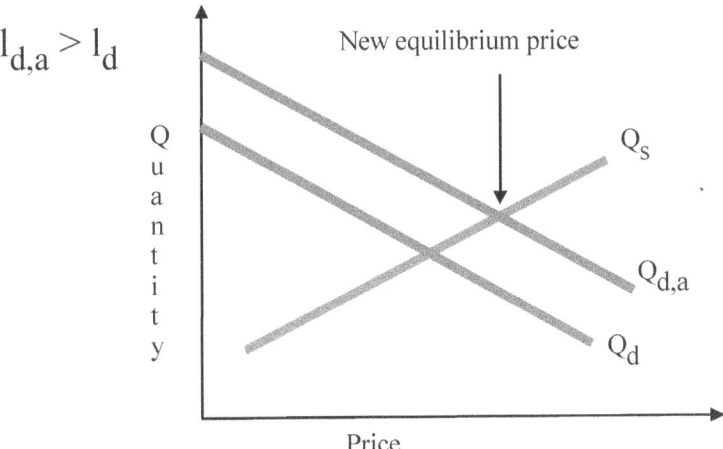

Figure 8 Advertising makes the price go up.

Again, we see that the customer has to pay more but gets the same product. And even that may be untrue. If advertising can be used to sell more even if the product is made of lower quality that is an option that will also increase the profits of a company. Thus, advertising could lead to the consumer paying more for a product that is not as good. Is this what we want? Not if we want to create more total trealth in a society.

Technology

We have previously argued for the enormous impact new ideas, new technology, has on trealth. How it changes the demand-supply situation is both easy and complex to predict. Naturally increasing technology should lead to an increase of supply. This is after all the basic result of the industrialisation. Thus:

$$Q_{s,t} = f_s(P,T), \qquad \frac{\partial f_s(P,T)}{\partial t} > 0$$

And given the same price:

$$Q_{s,t} > Q_s$$

Where the produced quantity is $Q_{s,t}$ after an increase in technology
and the quantity before this increase in use of technology was Q_s.
　　We had the $Q_s = k_s P + l_s$ equation for Q_s. So we can write this
equation for $Q_{s,t}$:

$$Q_{s,t} = k_{s,t}P + l_{s,t}$$

And using $Q_{s,t} > Q_s$ we get:

$$k_{s,t}P + l_{s,t} > k_s P + l_s$$

To simplify this we again take two cases, $l_{s,t} = l_s$ and $k_{s,t} = k_s$
respectively. The first case is shown in Figure 9. Because $l_{s,t} = l_s$ we
get:

$$k_{s,t}P + l_{s,t} > k_s P + l_{s,t}$$

Simplifying this by removing $l_{s,t}$ and dividing with P we get:

$$k_{s,t} > k_s$$

This just means that as price goes up, supply will, at a given price,
increase faster when more technology is used but expressed in
mathematical terms so we can draw our lines. See Figure 9.

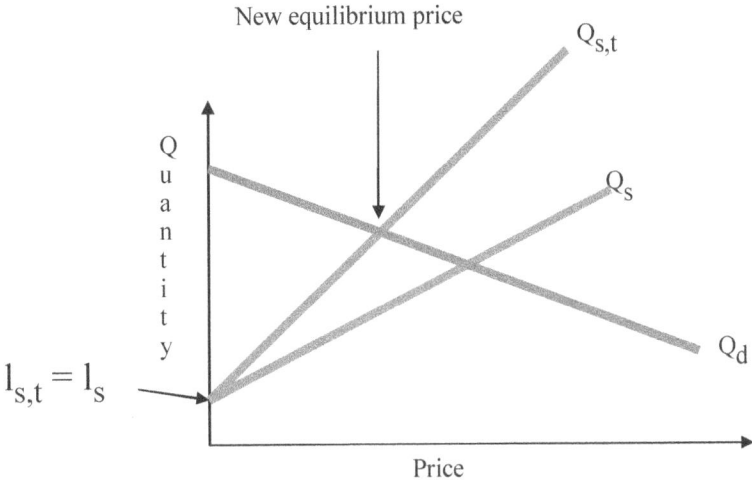

Figure 9 Better technology makes the price go down.

This is nothing strange, after all some technology made it possible to produce more shoes than when they were handmade and today machinery makes it possible to produce even more.

Thus, more technology gives us the same product at a lower price. However, the complexity with technology hinted at earlier lies with the fact that technology could influence both Q_s and Q_d. Increasing technology can lead to more interesting and competitive products, thus increasing **both** supply and demand. On the other hand we could then argue that we have another product and that we are discussing another Q_d.

Setting $k_{s,t} = k_s$ leads to a similar solution, we get a lower equilibrium price. This is left as an exercise to the reader. (I have always wanted to say that!)

Financial Markets

It may be that the models describe earlier, the "law" of supply and the "law" of demand, work fairly well for wheat and potatoes but as we saw earlier other factors such as advertisement may influence buyers to a greater extent than price. Also, why are hamburger restaurants such as McDonalds still selling french fries drenched in fat? This may produce profits but it surely is not good for society at large. And why did General Motors stop the production of EV1? Today when this is written there is a major crisis in the car industries in for example USA. The EV1 was the first modern production electric car from a major automaker (General Motors). The EV1 worked quite well but for obscure reasons the EV1 was discontinued 1999 with all such cars subsequently removed from the roads and destroyed. What had happened if General Motors had instead started a major project perhaps together with other major car producers aimed at producing electric cars? I tell you, instead of a major crisis they would today have had a new major technology to sell over the whole world and no such crisis.

I think we must describe these two examples as inefficient allocations of goods – that is, market failures! However when the models used to describe supply and demand for ordinary goods and services are transferred to financial markets becoming the theory of efficient capital markets, we get into real trouble. The restoring forces (higher price results in lower demand etc) that are supposed to go in the opposite direction from an initial change (and by that regulate the system) do not work at all! This is so because the stereotype mentioned earlier that says "expensive = good" seems to be at work here with extreme force:

> "When the price increases, it is common to observe, not a decrease but an increase in demand! Indeed, the rising price means a higher return for those who own the security, because of the capital gain. The price increase thus attracts new buyers, which further reinforces the initial increase. The promise of bonuses pushes traders to further strengthen the movement."[38]

This goes on until it all crashes. Hardly a case of sensible prices! The way financial markets are allowed to function today hardly leads to any kind of efficiency. Instead they become a permanent source of instability with huge fluctuations of exchange rates and of the stock market which are clearly unrelated to the fundamental needs of the

---

[38] Manifesto of the appalled economists. Real-world economics review, issue no.54.

economy. That is, with prices that have been disconnected from the true values, the trealth values, of things. This instability spreads to the rest of the economy through many mechanisms and "is evident from the uninterrupted series of bubbles that we have known in the past 20 years: Japan, South-East Asia, the Internet, emerging markets, real estate and securitization."[39]

Summary

The idea of demand and supply is an idea used a lot by economists. It says that, in a competitive market, price will move to an equilibrium price where there is no shortage and no waste. This is then seen as obviously very good.

However this disregards the morals of the situation. Yes, the market will reach an equilibrium price where as much dental care is produced that can be paid for by the members of a society. But surely, there will still be a real shortage of dental care because not all those that need it will get it! Only as much as the members are able to pay for will be produced. What type of nice equilibrium is that? Thus, this argument that at the equilibrium level there is no waste proposed as an objective neutral "fact," taught in schools and dominating the thoughts of most every economist is in reality a very political and biased argument. It is not an objective argument at all.

Also the price is only one of many factors that influence the demand and supply. We took two examples of this and using the tools the economists themselves use showed how advertising increases the price and how technology will decrease the price.

Finally we discussed how the direct transposition of these flawed theories (of demand and supply) when they have been transferred to the financial market has resulted in ridiculous prices and continued instability.

In short, the models used by the economists are just Cialdini shortcuts leaving out much of the details needed if we are to build a decent society.

---

[39] Manifesto of the appalled economists. Real-world economics review, issue no.54.

Economic Bubbles

> *No servant can serve two masters. Either he will hate the one and love the other, or he will be devoted to the one and despise the other. You cannot serve both God and Money.*
> *[Luke 16:13]*

The Market Value

The market price is set by the market in a complicated process where people interact in confusing ways. People need (or are at least persuaded to think they need) things. Other people produce things.

Advertising, trends, dreams, chance, direct manipulations, ignorance, greed and the full setup of human failings and strengths influence this process in difficult to see ways to finally produce a purchase (or not) at some price. This vast process of perplexing bewilderment is modelled by economist by the naive model discussed in chapter "Demand and Supply" and summarized again in Figure 10.

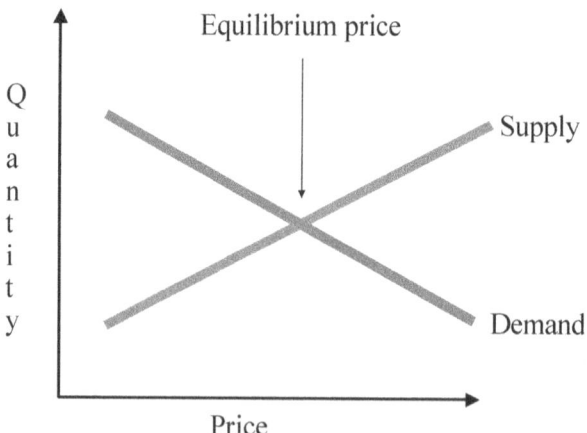

Figure 10 The market price as a function of demand and supply in a market.

We can summarize Figure 10 with this formula:

$market\ price = f(demand, supply)$

Such simple demand-supply reasoning's make economists very
happy. Should we be happy with this too?

Nope. To begin with economists like to put price and quantity in
the opposite way as shown in Figure 11. But this is just to confuse us
so it is no big deal. Also the supply and demand lines need not be
straight but can be more or less curved but this does not matter much
either. Worse is that if we let the market decide price in this way for
everything it means that many people that need for instance medical
or dental care will not get that because they cannot pay the price
demanded for such services. So all is not well at all whatever the
economists says about this.

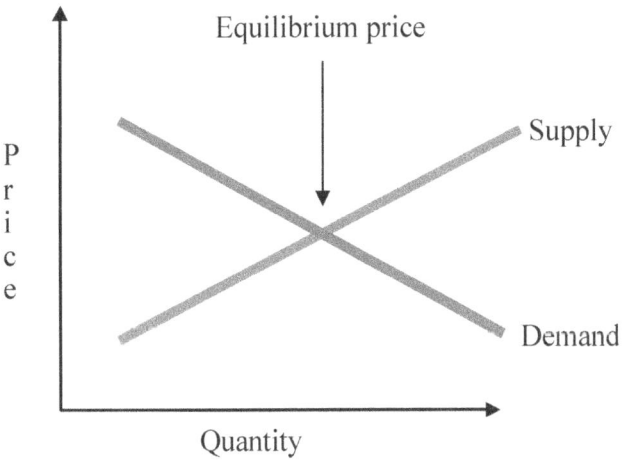

Figure 11 Price as function of quantity, a traditional equilibrium
calculation.

So to conclude, the supply-demand idea is a well known simple theory
of how the market price is set and as such it has it uses. But this model
is misleading because it does not make us focus on building trealth but
to focus on P, the price input. But this input is just one input of many.

The major problem of this model is thus that it makes us focus on money instead of true worth. So let's focus on something else!

The Barter Value

The barter value is the intrinsic value of a product or service that reflects the utilitarian qualities of the product or service. As pointed out earlier the "intrinsic" is the fundamental property that is reflected in the barter value. Intrinsic value in the sense "belonging to a thing by its very nature." A barter value represents the true worth, the trealth value, of something.

The big question is of course: "What is a correct barter price?" This has been a problem at least since the tulip mania in the Netherlands during the Dutch Golden Age (roughly spanning the 17th century). It so happened that the bulbs of the newly-introduced tulip became so popular that the price for them reached higher and higher values until they were extremely highly priced and then suddenly it all collapsed. This was perhaps the first economic bubble of significance. The bizarre market price was of course known for the bulbs even when it reached staggering heights but what about the barter value?

Yes, what is the difference between a market value and a barter value/price for something such as a house? The difference is that because the barter price is based on trealth it is a sensible value, a value within reason, and as such it is related to the cost of constructing the house.

The barter value cannot run away like the market price because we do not allow an endless supply of new bubble money to inflate it. We simply do not allow bad inventions such as the fractional reserve system for the barter value. It is then not possible for banks to create more bubble money for the barter value by giving loans much higher than they should.

The barter value can be seen as a modernized version of the **rentenmark** issued in Germany 1923, spearheaded by Hjalmar Schacht, to stop the hyperinflation that occurred in Germany after the First World War. In Germany, workers were paid twice per day and would shop as fast as possible to avoid further depreciation of their earnings. Shopkeepers stopped updating prices and instead showed a multiplier showing what the prices should be multiplied with. The Rentenmarks were issued in a fixed amount and were backed by hard assets such as mortgaged land and industrial goods worth 3.2 billion rentenmark. By strictly limiting currency supplies run-away increases of prices and wages stopped because there were then no money available to support higher prices and wages.

The main difference between the rentenmark and the (total) barter value available in a country is that it should be computed in a more complex way and updated year by year, taking into account our high-tech society and it should also include the worth of services.

The barter value will thus not vary as much over time as a market value because it is fixed by this connection to existing assets (including services) in a society. In the illustrating example in Figure 12 we can see that the market value and the barter value may start out at about the same level.

When we stand gaping at shares that go from 10 SEK to 200 SEK and then back again to 30 SEK or when a house doubles in price in a short time we instinctively know something is wrong. Economic models such as the one of demand and supply then short circuit our ability to apply common sense. The barter price as shown in Figure 12 on the other hand honours our common sense.

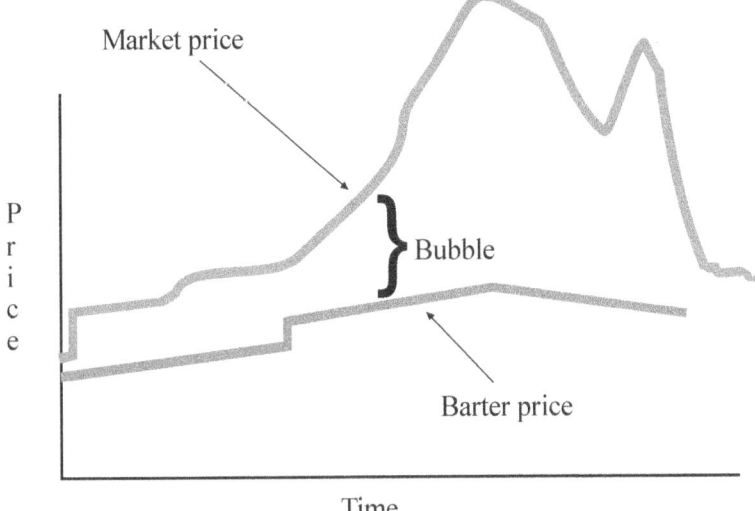

Figure 12 Example, market and barter price development for a house.

The barter price is an idea of a price that:

1. Honours our common sense by making us put down our feet
    and refuse to accept these extreme variations in price over
    time.
2. Demands that the price must be related to our concrete
    physical reality. That is, there must be something there – a
    commodity or a service – that backs up the barter money in an
    honest way. For instance by being related to the true cost of
    creating it. It is a value based on the trealth concept. See also
    chapter *Mapping Reality to a Model*. The exact calculation is
    of course not easy and is best left to experts just like with the
    rentenmark.
3. And, following directly from 2), it is related to a money
    supply without bubble money

For most things we can understand the barter price from the difficulty
in getting something, constructing or reconstructing something. We
can know this price by using what has more or less become outlawed
in the economic community, common sense. For instance gold in this
sense does not get its barter price from the scarcity of it but from the
actual cost of digging up a new piece of gold. A house gets it barter
price not from a set market price in a hot or cold market but from the
costs involved in building it. However, even here we may run into
some problems if the prices of, for instance, some or all of the
building materials are overpriced. However, we can know that there
exists a correct barter price even if we cannot set it exactly in this
book and this is important information by itself because then we can
make models of what is going on such as show in our illustrating
example in Figure 12.

We all know that the market values of things vary. In the case of
houses and shares the market value (price) may fluctuate a lot. The
trealth value (barter price) also varies as indicated. Why? It may be
that a house decays because it is not properly maintained or because
the neighbourhood turns sour. Then we do not want that house as

much and its barter value goes down just like the market value. Or it may be the reverse, we add a garage or a room to the house or there pops up a lot of nice shops in the neighbourhood, then we will have a higher barter value.

The first bump up in the market price in Figure 12 is when the constructor decided to sell the house at a higher cost than it took him to construct it.

The barter value is a more or less straight line going slowly up. It too has a bump up after some years when a room was added to the house. The barter line then goes slightly up for some time and then peeks and starts to go down. It starts to go down because the new owners did not care as much about maintaining the house so its utility/trealth value goes down. The market value fluctuates a lot more than the barter value.

The difference between the barter value and the market value is the bubble money:

house bubble = market value for house − barter value for house

We had earlier introduced this equation:

$$\sum_{all} money = \sum_{all} barter\ money + \sum_{all} bubble\ money$$

We can rewrite it like this:

$$\sum_{all} bubble\ money = \sum_{all} money - \sum_{all} barter\ money$$

Since the money here really is the money in our market system we can equally say this:

$$\sum_{all} bubble\ money = \sum_{all} market\ money - \sum_{all} barter\ money$$

In Figure 12 the bubble value is always positive (greater than zero). In Figure 13 we show how we can model this. In Figure 13 we have two new functions:

$u(s) = util\ value\ of\ s\ (something)$

$m(s) = market\ value\ of\ s\ (something)$

The first function called "u" describes how one input thing (the big house or small company as shown in the figure) is related to one value in our range of utility values (the world of true wealth, trealth). "u" is thus short for "utility." Note, in the ellipses we only show some sample values.

The other function "m" which is short for "market" shows the market value for the house. This function "m" is thought by the economists to be able to set the market value according to how we described it earlier. (See Figure 10 and Figure 11).

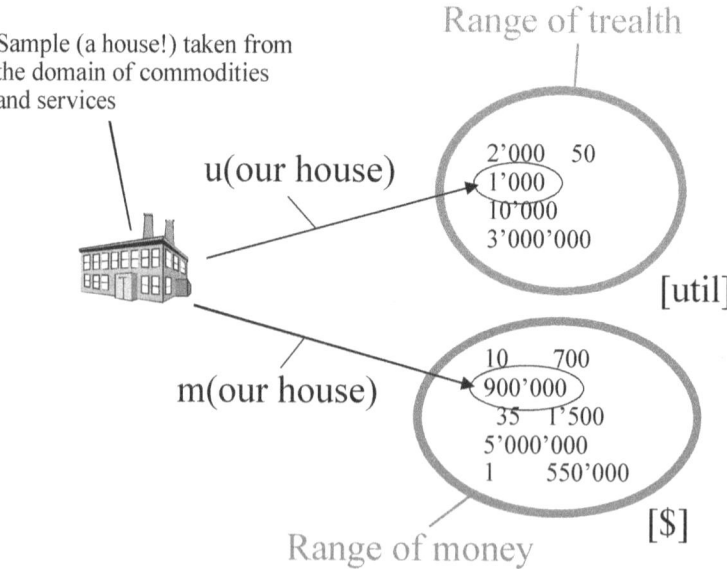

Figure 13 Trealth and market price.

If we input our particular house (here just called "our house") these equations yield the following values in our example:

$$u(our\ house) = 1000\ util$$

$$m(our\ house) = 900'000\ \$$$

We thus input one item (our house) in the function u which gives one output value, the 1000 util which is our value for the utility, how much trealth we have.

In the same way the function m gives one output value, the 900'000\$, [40] when we input our house in that function.

The words **domain** and **range** in Figure 13 are actually chosen with some care. A domain of a function is namely the set of input values for which a function is defined (that is, can be used for). And the range of a function is the set of all output values that a function can produce. In our case the domain (the input values) are the commodities and the services we talked about earlier for both u and m. The range of u is the possible util values. The range of m is the possible money values.

---

[40] The money could of course have been in any currency such as £ or SEK. We can define m for our choosing of currency or alternatively use several market functions for different currencies: $m_£$, $m_\$$, m_{SEK} and so forth.

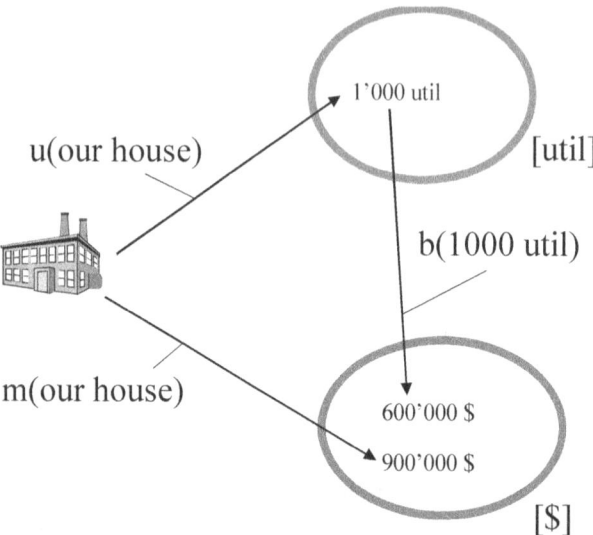

Figure 14 Trealth and market price and connecting them.

In Figure 14 we have simplified Figure 13 a bit by taking away the sample values and only kept those that we have in our example. We have also used the barter function *b* introduced in chapter *Trealth and Technology*. This is a function that relates a util value to the money world. That is, it shows how much barter value our 1000 util has when converted to money [$].

$b(1000\ util) = 600'000\ \$$

But hey, what is going on here? Why do we only get 600'000 $ when the house (or company) is worth 900'000 $? The mystery is explained in Figure 15.

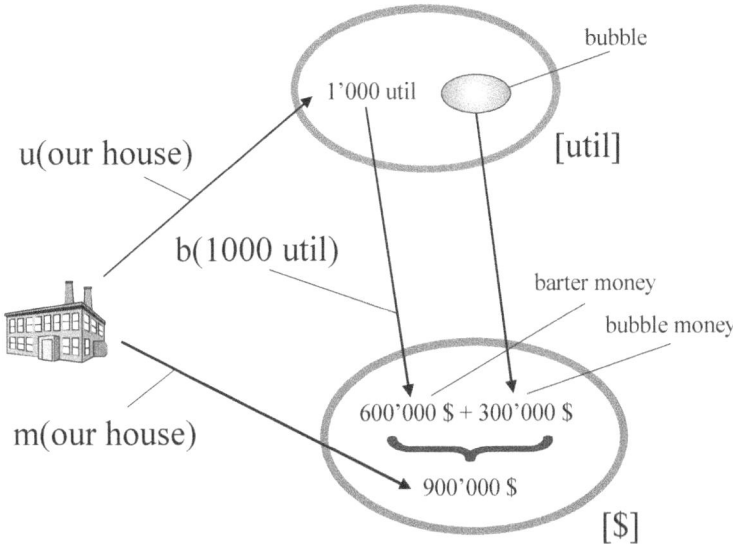

Figure 15 Explaining the difference between trealth and market prices with a bubble.

The market said the house was worth 900'000 $ but it is not really worth that much! The market tricked us and we have a bubble. Remember:

$$\sum_{all} market\ money = \sum_{all} barter\ money + \sum_{all} bubble\ money$$

That was when we summed over all items in a society. For or house we have:

900'000$ [*money*]
$$= 600'000\$ \ [barter\ money]$$
$$+ \ 300'000\$ \ [bubble\ money]$$

This was a rather small bubble, 50% of the utility value. If we had shares (or tulips, remember the tulip mania in the Netherlands) the bubble could be much bigger than this. The sky is the limit! Or rather

the limit is how inventive our financial geniuses are in inventing
schemes to create more bubble money.

When will a Bubble Burst?

The problem with letting the market function set prices is thus highly
related to the fact that bubble money can be created by banks and
other actors. See also chapters *Bubble Money and Barter Money* and
The Fractional Reserve System. This "extra" bubble money makes it
possible for the market price to run away to new highs.

   If the total sum of money was limited in some reasonable way to
the sum total of real value in a society this would not be possible. This
is exactly where the idea of barter money comes in. Of course it is not
possible to determine the sum total of barter money exactly down to
the last digit but to keep letting a very bad function, the market
function $m(i)$, set prices because we do not have a perfect
replacement is of course exceedingly foolish, close to madness.

   When do we have a bubble and when do we not have a bubble?
Small variations should not be considered bubbles but where do the
limit go? No problem we set up a rule. We have a bubble for an item i
when this is true:

$$\frac{m(i) - b(u(i))}{b(u(i))} > k_i$$

$i = item\ of\ interest$

$m(i) = market\ function\ giving\ us\ the\ market\ price\ for\ i\ in\ [money]$

$u(i) = utility\ function\ giving\ us\ the\ utility\ value\ for\ i\ in\ [util]$

$b(some\ [util])$
$= barter\ function\ giving\ us\ the\ [money]\ value\ for\ this\ [util]$

$k_i = threshold\ level\ for\ item\ i$

This means that when the difference between the market value and the real (barter) value is larger than a given threshold we have a bubble.

That is, the **threshold** is the point at which a further increase in the market value will make enough people realize the foolishness of the market price so that a panic can start. That is, when even a small increase in the market value represents a stimulus of sufficient intensity to begin to produce (with high probability) an effect, in our case *the bubble effect; the market value is so high that it will (with high probability) crash*. I leave it to the reader to set a correct value for k_i.

Personally I think that perhaps a *k* value of 0.5 is a rather reasonable limit for many items. A *k* value of 0.5 means that we have an overprice relative *b(u(i))* of 50%. If we cannot talk about a bubble then, when can we?

If we want to be a bit more advanced we can do this by introducing different stages:

- a pre-bubble stage (it is close to becoming a bubble, k > 0.3),
- it is a bubble (k > 0.5),
- it is a big bubble (can burst anytime, k > 1),
- it is a critical bubble (should have burst by now, k > 3). [41]

Interestingly the bubbles can be negative too. We can have a hole! This can happen when for instance a large company is sold at less than what its parts are worth. A smart capitalist can then buy the company and sell out its parts making a handsome profit equal to the negative bubble without creating anything usable to share with his fellow citizens. Figure 16 illustrates this.

In Figure 16 the market value for the company is only 450'000 $ but the parts of it are really worth 600'000 $. Thus by buying the company for 450'000 $ and selling the parts for 600'000 $ someone can make a profit of 150'000 $ without contributing anything of worth (trealth) to the real world.

---

[41] Of course, these values, are mostly for illustrations. Finding the true values are left to the reader as an exercise. (How I do love to say that!)

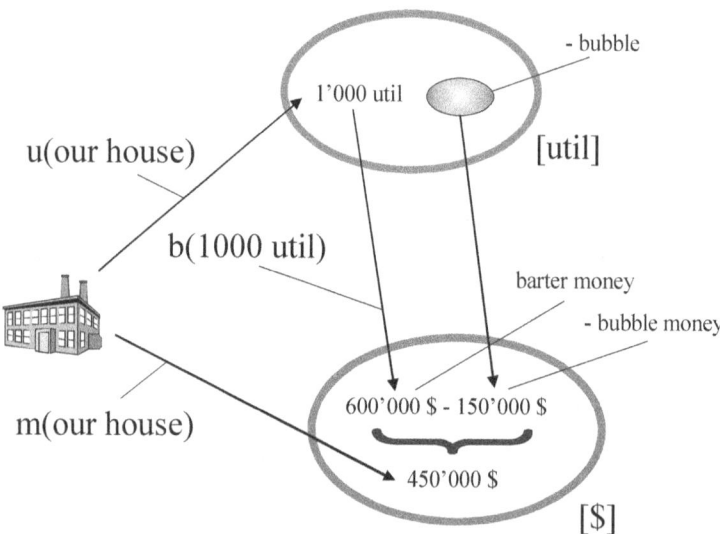

Figure 16 Bubbles can be negative. They then represent hidden values in something.

If we want an equation that tells us when we have a hole we can write it like this, we have a negative bubble, a hole when:

$$\frac{b(u(i)) - m(i)}{b(u(i))} > k_i$$

(We must put *b(u(i))* first because we want the left side to be positive.)

If we introduce the | | function [42] we can write a general formula like this that is valid both for bubbles and holes:

$$\frac{|m(i) - b(u(i))|}{b(u(i))} > k_i$$

---

[42] The absolute value of a number is the value without regard to its sign. So, for example, 7 is the absolute value of both 7 and −7. In programming languages this is often called abs. That is abs(-7) = 7 and abs(7) = 7. In mathematics however this is denoted by | |. That is, |-7| = 7 and |7| = 7.

Bubbles - a Way of Stealing

Figure 17 shows how the market value varies a lot for something with a trealth value that does not vary much with time because the trealth value is the intrinsic value. It could be shares or houses or something else. It becomes a matter of buying at the right time – when the market price is below the trealth barter value – and selling when the market value is above the barter price. The better we can buy or sell at the right time the more we "earn" but no trealth, is created. The perspective is wrong.

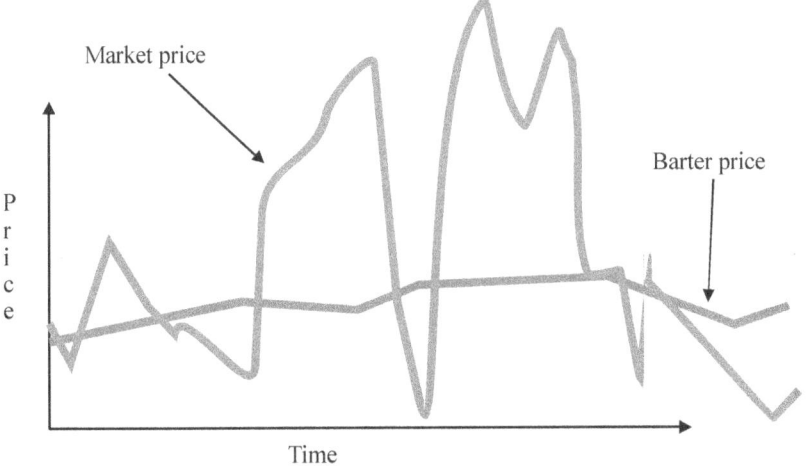

Figure 17 Market and trealth (barter) price example.

Creativity, energy and time are spent on speculation, inventing new economic schemes and creating sophisticated advertising instead of increasing our ability to create trealth through new technology. We maximize profits [money] but not trealth [util] which is the only honest way to go. Our slogan should be "*Much less of speculation and much more of innovation.*"

Since it becomes a matter of being able to sell or buy at the right moment and this does not create any new trealth but just transfers the right of trealth it resembles lottery or stealing. When you steal you transfer the ownership just like you do here. Thus today the economic schemes are like a legal way of stealing.

Summary

The supply-demand idea is a much used well known simple theory of how the market price is set. However, this model is grossly misleading because it does not make us focus on building trealth but to focus on price.

The barter value is the intrinsic value of something and as such much better represents the true value of something. It is a sensible value, a value within reason, and as such it is related to the cost of making something. The barter value will also not vary as much over time as a market value because we do not allow any bubble money to inflate it.

The problem with letting the market function set prices is highly related to the fact that money can be created by banks and other actors. This "extra" bubble money makes it possible for the market price to run away to new highs. If the total sum of money was limited in some reasonable way to the sum total of real value in a society this would not be possible.

We also illustrated the idea of a "bubble" which is the difference between the market value and the true value of something. We used this formula

$$\sum_{all} bubble\ money = \sum_{all} market\ money - \sum_{all} barter\ money$$

And had an example of a bubble for a house:

$$house\ bubble = market\ value\ for\ house - barter\ value\ for\ house$$

Today the economic schemes are a way of legal robbery. The thing becomes a matter of buying at the right time – when the market price is below the trealth barter value – and selling when the market value is above the barter price instead of creating true wealth, trealth.

Modeling Basics

Look to the essence of a thing, whether it be a point of doctrine, of practice, or of interpretation. [Marcus Aurelius Antonius]

Good modeling is essential to getting usable models. Here I add a few words about that subject. [43] Let us start by defining a few important concepts.

A **system** is an assemblage of things (including facts, principles, doctrines, or the like) forming an often complex whole where the combination of the parts yields something new, the system. For instance, the digestive system, system of government, "society," a computer system or a scheme of classification such as the Linnaean system.

A **model** represents a system in graphic and narrative form. **Modeling** is the act of creating a model. **The world** is everything in our universe. The part of the world in which we take an interest is our **reality**. A word sometimes used for this is **UoD** (Universe of Discourse). The way we go about modeling follows a **methodology** which simply is the set of rules, practices, concepts, and procedures we apply to a specific branch of knowledge. Or in simpler words, a methodology is the ideas we follow to create a model.

The most important principle when modeling in physics and other fields of true science is that if a model does not work, it does not yield the results we expect and want, then it must be revised. That is, in a nutshell, the main argument in this book why we must scrap current economic models. The way economists view the world simply do not give us what we truly deep in our hearts need, trealth, true wealth. Instead they just transfer more and more money into the pockets of the already too rich.

---

[43] Much of the text here is taken from my book Understanding Object-Oriented Software Engineering published by IEEE Press 1996. That book deals in a more complete way with the subject of modeling but specializes in modeling when we are building complex software systems.

It is high time that the economists should have to face the same stern questions as engineers, physicists and scientists in all fields of true science must constantly answer: "*Does it work? Do the models give us what we need and want?*" If the answer is "no", it does not work, then there is an imperative need to use others models and concepts.

Apart from this basic common sense principle that a model must work in the sense that it yields results that we feel comfortable with, what is important when we go about modeling? I will here take up some other important factors for getting usable models.

Mapping Reality to a Model

> *Everything should be made as simple as possible, but not one bit simpler.[Albert Einstein]*

The mapping between reality and our model should be simple and straightforward. Why is this simple mapping so important? To answer that question, let us recall the paradox about the male barber who shaved everyone in his little village who did not shave themselves and only those people. **With this sentence we have built a little model of reality**, but we have a problem: Who shaves the barber?

- If he shaves himself, he is not allowed to shave himself, because he did not shave those who shaved themselves.
- On the other hand, if he does not shave himself, he should shave himself, because he is supposed to shave everyone who does not shave himself.

Is this paradox a problem? In reality, there is not a problem, because the beard on the barber will grow longer and longer unless someone cuts it!

That is, the real world does not tolerate paradoxes. The world is inerrant—infallible—*and the problem is to be found in our model, because it does not describe the situation properly.*

What we learn from this little example is that we must never let the model become our reality. This is however exactly what has happened when the economists today have been allowed to define reality for us. But reality is not the money model, the demand and supply model and so on. If a model does not help us or puts us in some impossible situation like the model of the barber – or the models of the economists today – we must break free and build other models that give us what we want; True wealth, those things that are useful to us.

Naming

> *The chief merit of language is clearness, and we know that nothing detracts so much from this as do unfamiliar terms. [Galen]*

One of the most neglected ways of bringing about a good model is to give good names to the things we put into the model. If we give good names our model will be understandable in an easy manner. The extra time spent on finding good names is well-spent effort. A name should feel right. Trust your instinct. Finding good names is an iterative process. If a first try does not produce satisfactory results, try again later.

Thus a word we introduce should add to the easy understanding of something. I choose the word trealth because it is easy to connect that with the idea of true wealth. Viewed this way, the enormous proliferation of obscure economic concepts that has appeared serves only one real purpose, to make it difficult to understand what is going on. And even worse, we become bound by these concepts and because of that we become blind and unable to break free. To break free from the prison economists have created in our minds we need new concepts and they start with new names. Thus, we need new concept such as true wealth, trealth.

The Importance of Purpose

> *The secret of success is constancy to purpose. [Benjamin Disraeli, Earl of Beaconsfield]*

We find a lot of things when modeling—but what do we find? Let us describe a book.

A possible approach would be to describe a book as consisting of *covers* with several *pages* between them. Each page is then described as made up of several *lines*, sometimes including *pictures*. Each line can be described as a series of *characters* and (possibly) *digits*.

Another view could be more logical: The book contains several *chapters*. Each chapter has one or several *subchapters*. A subchapter might contain smaller *subchapters* (and *headers*), until we find *paragraphs*. A paragraph is made up by grouping one or several *sentences*. Sentences and headers are made up by grouping *words* and *numbers*. A word is made up by one or more *characters* and a number is made up of one or more *digits*.

The two views, one physical and one logical, gave two different models. Behind each view hides a unique purpose. Various purposes thus yield different models when we describe something. The point here is that there is not one model – such as the economic models in popular use today that defines something in an objective and neutral way. Rather it is the other way around, we have a purpose when we model and that yields the model. Take a computer system for instance. To a systems analyst, a system consists of jobs, programs, files, etc. A user would probably regard the system as something composed of reports, computer terminals, screens, etc.

A good design rule is to take the user's perspective using the user's words and his or her definitions and understandings of the meaning of those words. The more exact our purpose is defined and the more uniform our understanding of something is, the more alike our models will be.

When it comes to building a good society we are the users. It is our needs and desires taken together that should define the purposes of the models used. Not the need of the economists or the greedy. Now take that to your heart!

Defining the purpose is thus the key. A famous example that illustrates that there is always a purpose hiding whenever we try to model reality is the discussions about the nature of fundamental particles (i.e., electrons, protons, neutrons, etc.) that took place early in the 20th century. It became evident that the particles did not always behave as something that had a well-defined shape and size—that is, as something we would call particles (see Figure 18).

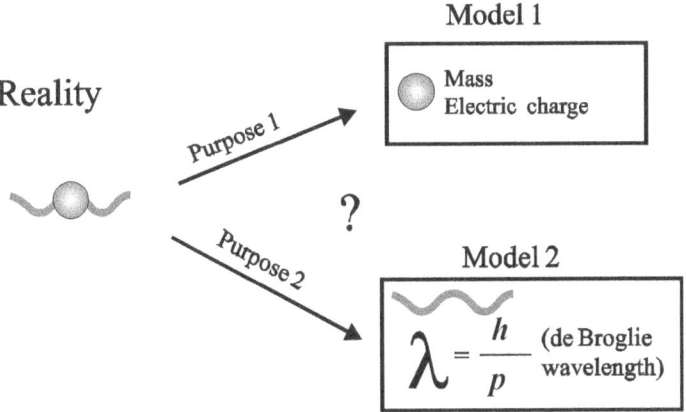

Figure 18 Is an electron a wave or a particle? What about a proton?

Apparently, the fundamental particles in some experiments behaved as particles with characteristics like mass and electric charges, whereas in other experiments they behaved as waves producing diffraction patterns. It was found that the model needed to explain an experiment *depended on the intent, the purpose of the experiment.*

A way for us to explain this problem is to say that reality is our only complete model. When we build a model to explain something, we get a fragmentary model. If we are lucky, this model will suit our purpose but probably not much more. We can state this explanation in another way: The model we make will be a true abstraction because it does not include every detail from reality. Figure 19 illustrates this in a more general way. The figure shows how our purpose governs our selection when we look at reality and decide what we shall include in a model.

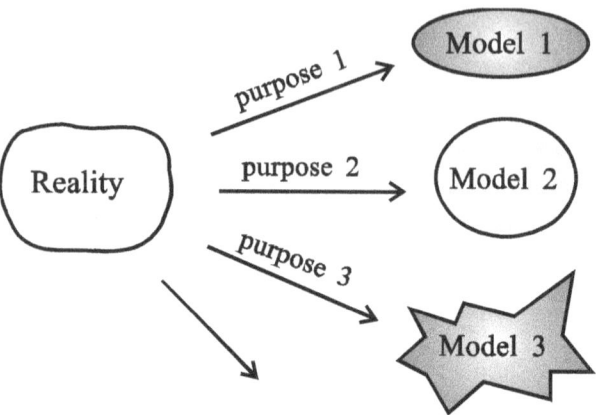

Figure 19 How reality is modelled depends on the purpose.

Figure 20 is an example illustrating the principle in Figure 19. Describing the orbit of a satellite would yield one model, and describing the heat balance of the same satellite would yield another model. A third and different model would have to be used if we wanted to describe the chances of the satellite being destroyed by another orbiting satellite.

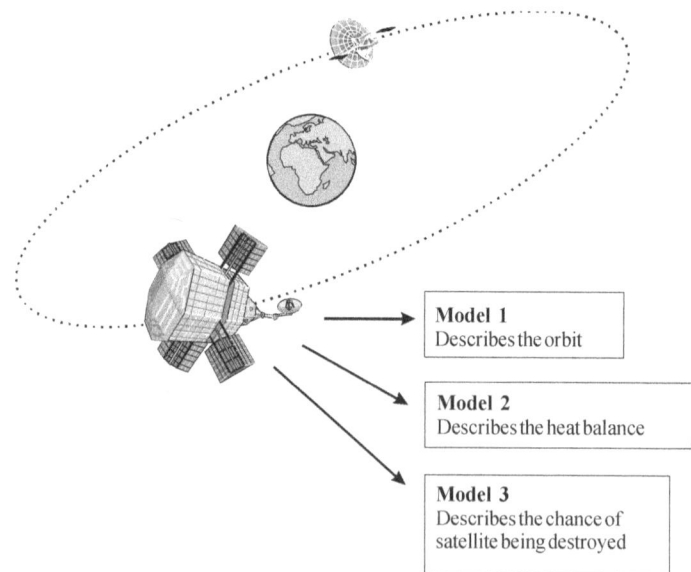

Figure 20 To describe a satellite, we need several different models.

Another example is shown in Figure 21. If we want to keep track of hardware parts in an inventory system, we need a model for this purpose. With this purpose (keeping track of hardware parts) we will need details that can be described with the inventory number, price, type, etc.

An engineering department at the same company that use the same sensor to take temperature readings in some machinery will need other attributes and they will also need to describe the functionality of the sensor. This results in a completely different model as shown in the bottom of Figure 21.

Each purpose thus also here results in a different model even though the object of interest, the sensor, was the same.

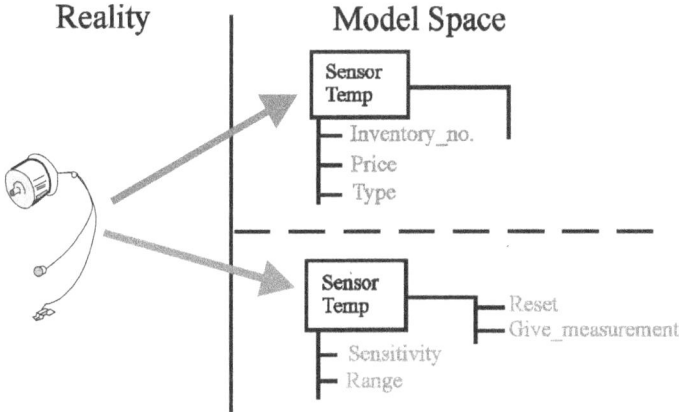

Figure 21 Different purposes yields different needs of details in a model.

Purposes and Economic Models

> *When we build, let us think that we build forever. [John Ruskin]*

If the purpose is not defined well enough by those who design a model, confusion or even disaster will result. The economists are as it seems not even aware of this fact. They do not understand that there are hidden purposes behind the models they use.

The all important conclusion we must reach is then that we should never allow economists to define the purpose for us. The consequence of a selected purpose is much too important for us to allow the selection of the purpose to be put in the hands of the economists! This is simply so because the purpose is not defined by the economists as maximizing trealth by maximizing the amount of new ideas but instead they focus on price – money. It is exactly here that the economists make one of their cardinal errors. They act as if their models – in particular the money model – can be used to measure everything, even what we want to have, trealth. But we need different units for different things.

It is ok to use pounds to measure the weight of potatoes or even people but if we want to measure the weight of ships with pounds we find that it is not a good idea and we turn to the concept of tonnage instead. Why? Of course because we have different needs. We could say, the purpose of "pounds" is to measure the weight of things where it works well when we try to understand the weight. But weighing ships with pounds does not give us what we need, an understanding of how much a ship can carry. Instead we use a concept called tonnage [44] for this.

And how should we measure the distance between Stockholm and New York with pounds? Or the distance to the sun or to other stars? Or the temperature of something? This is of course nonsense!

To think that economic models centred on money can be used to create and measure trealth is like believing that pounds can be used for measuring the distance between New York and Stockholm.

The purpose of the money model is to ease the exchange of the products and services we produce and for this the money model is usable but if the purpose is to increase true wealth, trealth, we need to create models for that instead. Then we need models that lead us to greater trealth. We show this in Figure 22. The purpose "Help us barter efficiently" gives us the money model. The purpose "Help us

---

[44] The tonnage of a ship is the cargo volume of a ship. The actual tonnage is reached by a sometimes complex calculation. There are several variations of this measurement used to measure the capacity of a merchant vessel in different ways.

create more true wealth" surfaces the need of *other* models that can help us figure out how to create true wealth.

The same applies to Adam Smith's misinterpreted idea of the "invisible hand."

The supply-demand model has its uses as has been shown but it is really a very politically biased idea that will not give us the distribution of wealth that civilized societies want and need to prosper.

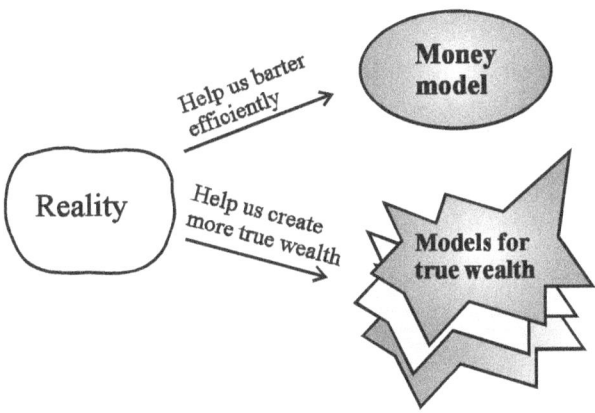

Figure 22 The money model cannot be used for everything. We also need radically different models.

Alternate models discussed in this book include the idea of trealth, economic bubbles, why we should not talk about scarce resources, source and support processes and how the idea of new ideas – new technology – as the fundamental enabling factor for more trealth ties all this together.

Summary

If a model does not work, it does not yield the results we expect and want, then it must be revised. The main argument in this book is that the models used by the economists do not work well because they do not give us what we truly deep in our hearts need.

The enormous proliferation of obscure economic concepts that has appeared serves only one real purpose, to make it difficult to understand what is going on. We become bound by these concepts and because of that we become blind and unable to break free. To break free from this prison of ideas we need new concepts and they start with new names. Thus, we need new concepts such as true wealth, trealth.

When it comes to building a good society it is our needs and desires taken together that should define the purposes of the models used. It is exactly here that the economists make one of their cardinal errors. The economists think they can use the same models (the money model, the supply-demand model, the invisible hand and so forth) to describe everything. But the purpose of the money model is to ease the exchange between us of the products and services we produce and for this the money model is excellent.

However, if the purpose is to increase true wealth, trealth, we need other models that can lead us to greater trealth. And, that is what this book is about!

Increasing Trealth

> *Whoever loves money never has money enough; whoever*
> *loves wealth is never satisfied with his income. This too is*
> *meaningless. [Eccl 5:10]*

Introduction

We do not want to have wealth in the "money" sense. We want to
have true wealth; Commodities and services that are of use to us and
that has been created in a human way.

The money idea, the demand and supply ideas and so forth, like
the top of an iceberg, are today misused and abused leading to a state
where we can rightly say that money is dishonest money and that we
are being lead along the wrong paths. We are made to go paths that do
not "capture the essence of a human being." Nor do we get good
utilitarian things.

So, where do we go from here? What can we do? We can hope
and pray that a paradigm shift will occur. That people will get so tired
of the situation that they will get so angry that they will be able to
stand up to the elite, those smart ones, those rich ones, those that
profit from the current elaborate system of transferring trealth to
themselves through all these economic schemes but without creating
any new trealth themselves.

But getting angry is not enough. As long as people are locked in
the present static way of bookkeeping economic thinking change is in
a sense impossible. It is impossible because we cannot go outside the
mind-set of ideas that we have been taught. This is very clear from
research such as the research done by researchers such as Professor
George Lakoff and Professor Robert Cialdini.

Only if other ideas and concepts explaining how true wealth is
produced are understood can a change occur. Thus only if we do
understand that money in no sense *is* true wealth but just a reflection
of it and that wealth that is not what we want to have (such as working
harder and faster and longer hours) is not true wealth can a change

begin. And only if models that explain the difference between wealth and true wealth, trealth, are understood can we break free. The moment we understand that the ideas of Adam Smith are just pure greed and selfishness and that there is a much better way to build a society based on true wealth do we have the tools necessary for starting a necessary change. Then and only then is it possible for a paradigm shift to occur.

Trealth and Technology

Trealth is directly connected to technology as we expressed with this argument:

$$P = p\big(l(H,T), g(H,T), tmg(H,T), m(H,T)\big), \qquad \frac{\partial p(H,T)}{\partial t} > 0$$

T has a very long and very successful history of having been increased with the result that productivity has increased. For instance productivity increased with 1'205% in USA, 3'396% in Japan and with 2'349% in Sweden between 1870 and 1990. [45]

The dependency on the input H is more complicated. After all H has actually decreased from a 6-7 day week with working hours of 12-14 hours every day to a 48 hour week and now a 40 hour week and still trealth has increased a lot.

Also, as has been pointed out earlier, increasing H is very difficult and could have a negative impact if increasing the workload leads to sick people or even "burnt out" people. Thus it should be clear to all (except perhaps economists and politicians) that the focus must be on increasing the amount of and power of technologies. It is the T factor that is the key to future trealth.

Thus the way to increase trealth is to make a society concentrate on maximizing the potential of human beings to come up with new ideas and then to maximize the opportunities for converting these ideas into new products and services.

---

[45] Sources: August Maddison, 1982, OECD 1991.

The Strict Father Model

Do you not know, my son, with what little understanding the world is ruled? [Pope Julius III]

If it is obvious that the key to a more prosperous society are new ideas why is the world not run the way to maximize the creation of and implementation of new ideas?

We can get some insight about this by connecting to the works of Professor George Lakoff. In his book *Moral Politics* he shows how much of the practical politics today is formed by two conflicting basic views, two different models of thought that he calls the **strict father model** and the **nurturant parent model** respectively.

The strict father model that dominates us today "assumes that life is struggle for survival. Survival in the world is a matter of competing successfully. . . . It is through competition that we discover who is moral. That is, who has been properly self-disciplined and therefore deserves success, and who is fit enough to survive and even thrive in a difficult world. Rewards given to those who have not earned them through competition are thus immoral. They violate the entire system." [46]

Clearly the focus here is on the abilities of individuals. This view of how a person should be is reflected in how the world should be. "The world must be and must remain a competitive place. . . —then what kind of a world is a moral world? It is necessarily one in which some people are better off than others, and they deserve to be. It is a meritocracy." [47] And of course to be able to be competing well you must be strong and "Anything that promotes moral weakness is immoral. If welfare (for instance) is seen as taking away the incentive to work and thus promoting sloth, then . . welfare is immoral." [48]

Tax cuts have in this system two good results. They reduce the possibility for welfare and it will reward the best people ". . . there will simply be little money available for social programs . . . It also rewards. . . 'the best people', according to Strict Father morality,

---

[46] *Moral Politics* by George Lakoff, Pages 67-68.
[47] *Moral Politics* by George Lakoff,.Page 69.
[48] *Moral Politics* by George Lakoff. Page 74.

namely, those who have used their discipline, engaged in competition, sought their self-interest, and become self-reliant (read wealthy)."[49]

At the core of this system we also find that "A mature adult becomes self-reliant through applying self-discipline in pursuing his self-interest." [50] Life is a though struggle where the individual must make it by him or herself and where the results can be measured in the amount of money someone has acquired. In this system we "believe that the rich are morally superior to the poor. . .The rich (who are disciplined and talented enough and who have worked hard enough to become rich deserve their wealth and the poor (either through lack of industry or talent) deserve their poverty." [51]

Being rich means having a lot of money and this thus directly connects to how we view ourselves. If we are rich we are morally superior. Not all of us agrees with this but would rather agree with for instance the catholic priest Richard Rohr who puts it like this:

> "I wonder if you have ever heard a single sermon in your life on the tenth commandment? . . . 'Coveting our neighbor's goods 'is now called shopping, advertising and contributing to the gross national product (GNP) and the American economy. Amazing how the capital sin of greed can be transmuted into a major virtue."[52]

This is how the world is run today and it explains why thoughts and efforts are not focused on getting more ideas and converting these to new products and services that are of true use to us. The emergence of new ideas – if someone even thinks about it – is assumed to occur automatically if the system is just set up in this competitive way where money is the goal, the measuring stick of morality and the means through which society should be shaped.

The focus is thus on "making" money – not on creating more trealth. To produce new good utilitarian things from new untested ideas we must embark on risky, often long term projects that are

---

[49] Moral Politics by George Lakoff, page 408.
[50] Moral politics, by George Lakoff. Page 66.
[51] Moral Politics by George Lakoff,.Pages 83-84.
[52] From wild man to wise man by Richard Rohr. Page 63.

invariably costly. Faced with such prospects "smart" people
understand that it is easier, faster and much more profitable to invent
more or less advanced economic schemes to create bubble money that
will transfer money to themselves. This occurs simply because money
is in focus and not trealth.

The outbreak of riots and protests we see today in Europe is also a
reflection of these two competing visions of what a society should be.
On the one hand there is a vision of a Europe following an emphatic
social welfare model. On the other hand there is a vision in Brussels
and many national governments of a Europe with reduced public
services and less of industrial policies and where we instead of
building a bulwark against liberal globalization should "adapt"
European economies to the "needs" of globalization.

This is the difference between a Christian emphatic society and a
brutal very individualistic society and where the struggle ends will
have long going consequences for us all.

A focus on money also makes it difficult to explain the very idea
of trealth. Wealth for many people means "money" or possibly gold
and jewellery. It then becomes difficult to explain that for instance
unpaid work has anything to do with "wealth" such as the work done
by leaders for boy and girl scouts, the work done by parents to raise
their children and so on. Those following the strict father model will
have great difficulty accepting such ideas because of their focus on
the one and only result that in their view should be counted: Money.

Enablers of Better Technology

How does new technology emerge? Is it the market? The demand and
supply that makes this happen? Economists would like us to believe
that. But this false belief is debunked if we just think a little about it
and look at our history.

The market would never have put a man on the moon. The market
would never have conquered Hitler. The market would never have
created the well-fare state we have had in Sweden.

It was the vision of one man, President John F Kennedy that put
the first man on the moon. It was the well-planned effort – something
far removed from the typical market situation - that made it possible

to use industries and people to create a fighting machine that could defeat Hitler. It was the dreams and hard work and sacrifice of many many people inspired and lead by other people such as Mäster Palm, Hjalmar Branting and Per-Albin Hansson that made the welfare state of Sweden a possibility.

It works the other way around too. If people such as Hitler can have their dreams realized we get a nightmare. If a good project like the EV1 is discontinued we may get a crisis. And in Sweden the welfare state is under attack by people such as Fredrik Reinfeldt and people suffer and some people commit suicide.

Thus, new good technology emerges when there are leaders that make it possible for thinkers, engineers and workers to create it, and use it to create new products and services. The market mechanism is there but it is more like a raw force that must be wielded to a good purpose. In the same sense as steam power is useless unless it is channelled through machinery to yield something we need. It is a power that can be wielded for good or bad but to create something usable it must be wielded.

But what are the enablers for increasing technology? I can see several ones, the insight of how true wealth is created by inspired (political) leadership and a low level of corruption so that positions go to the right people and so that decisions are made for the right reasons (and not because of bribes) for instance. Without such fundamental and crucial factors any effort to increase true wealth will be severely handicapped. Just look at Zimbabwe or remember Idi Amin in Uganda or see the poverty in many otherwise rich countries in Africa, Asia and South America for instance.

However, in this book we assume such factors operate well and we limit our perspective to factors more directly related to technology. So what factors could there be? Here are my suggestions:

People. Everyone must be empowered to the greatest possible level to generate new high-tech ideas. Thus a generous and free educational system that makes it possible for everyone to get a good education is essential. But it also means that society should constantly evaluate the current situation and ascertain what types of education we need now and tomorrow so that the level of technology can be raised. This means that the society should encourage those types of education that will do this best with incentives of different types.

Opportunity. It must be possible for creative people to realize their ideas. The traditional way of doing this is in companies but the key is really that there are opportunities for these people to realize their ideas and that their ideas can be taken into products and services. That this is traditionally done in companies of the types we have today does not necessitate that it need be like this in the future. Also as noted in chapter *Source and Support Processes* companies are not equal in their ability to create trealth. Thus companies based on new ideas and using a high-level of technology are to be preferred.

If it is easy and straightforward to start companies based on new ideas and get help with what is needed to start and run the companies, we will see more companies created.

If there is a good social security system more people will dare to start new companies. If there is help available to run these special "Idea companies" they will be more successful because today there are so many other things that distract the focus when developing an idea. Administration, keeping in contact with the tax authorities, knowing how to lead projects, marketing and so on are all necessary skills to run a company but why should they be necessary for someone with an idea? People with ideas must be helped with these practical things simply because the more the society can help make it easy to start and run companies based on new ideas, the more new ideas will be realized.

But it must be that new ideas are in focus. Another barber shop or taxi service that is just a copy of existing such companies will not yield as much trealth as companies based on new high-technology ideas.

New ideas and new companies should be regarded as new born babies, pampered, protected and made to grow up in a safe and nourishing environment.

Inspired leaders showing discernment. Those in power must understand the mechanisms and dependencies behind creating trealth and that they have a responsibility to create the right conditions for this process to function well. If we leave all to the free market and believe that the invisible hand will fix things the smart ones will get rich but most people will get slowly poorer and in the end such thinking can ruin a whole country.

Instead we need a process in several steps:

1. Create conditions so that the level of technology – the amount of good ideas – can increase maximally.
2. Make sure the new technology is used to implement new products and services. That is, ideas must be transferred into new products and services or the potential of them will not be realized.
3. Make sure new products and services, representing trealth, are produced in the country as much as possible. If they are manufactured in other countries much of the trealth will be created there instead.

A Hamburger Restaurant

Let's look at a simple example, a hamburger restaurant to illustrate how the focus on money or trealth leads to radically different developments.

The discussion here is applicable to a number of jobs such as stock-room workers, cleaners and so on but we select a hamburger restaurant to illustrate the consequences of being motivated by different focus.

When hamburger restaurants such as McDonalds started it was something new. A streamlined operation with a simple menu and a kitchen set up like an assembly line, to ensure maximum efficiency. New ideas started the success of hamburger chains such as McDonalds. But this was more than 50 years ago!

Today we have been exposed to what new technology can do and anyone that has been in a hamburger restaurant at rush hours cannot but wonder, where is the machinery that automates the work so that the employees do not have to run around as mad chickens manually making hamburgers, French fries and so on? Why is machinery to make these things, assemble them and put them into containers automatically not in place now? Why do customers still have to order what they want manually instead of via a terminal at the tables where they sit down? After all we live in the 21:Th century do we not? A lot has happened since McDonalds started out but not much has changed with their menu or their assembly line in the kitchen. Why?

The answer is simple, owners are out to maximize profits (money) and if that can be down by keeping salaries and taxes low that is much easier and more free from risk than starting new projects targeted at developing machinery that can automate manual tasks. Well, that approach is only less risk prone in the short run. Perhaps somebody should tell McDonalds about the fate of the ice-box when the refrigerator came?

Anyway, the owner of a business will look at different ways to increase profits. The most popular one today seem to be through keeping down salaries and taxes and through demanding that the workers shall work harder. This is practically risk free for the owners. Burnt out personnel can easily be replaced with new workers. It involves no great costs and it leads directly – at least over the short time – to greater profits. Introducing new technology is on the other hand very costly and connected to real risks. Few development projects are successful.

If our perspective is to maximize trealth everything becomes different. Then it is a much better thing if one employee in a 30 hour week can do the work two employees did before in 40 hour weeks. Then it becomes natural to follow the tradition of the industrial revolution and find ways so that each worked hour can produce more due to the impact of new ideas. The focus will be on increasing available technology – more ideas – that can enable the creation of more true wealth.

However, even if we follow this way, new trealth will not automatically be shared with employees and consumers. There is no natural law that makes this happen. Rather experience shows that profit will be maximized as long as that is possible without any sharing.

If the salaries in the hamburger restaurant example were 2X for the two employees working 40 hour weeks before automation there is a real risk that the employer does not even want to pay X in salary for 30 hours because 30 hours is less than 40 hours. Using the trealth perspective the argument is instead that the employer should pay more than X in salary for these 30 hours because in our example the employee is creating much more trealth. The natural compromise should be some mix where the savings – because there is only one salary to pay – should be split between employee, employer and the customer. After all this is what has happened over and over again if we look at things from a historical perspective.

However, such a development is not automatic but depends on moderating forces such as the moral system of the owner, the strength of unions, laws stating minimum wages and so forth. It all becomes a moral and political matter.

Summary

The focus on money in our society motivates smart people to spend time on inventing economic schemes to create bubble money so they can transfer ownership of existing trealth to themselves. In a sound society they would rather spend time on creating new ideas that could increase trealth for us all.

New good technology emerges when there are inspired leaders that have the insight to create an environment where it is easy for thinkers, engineers and workers to get ideas and develop them into new products and services.

Everyone must be empowered to the greatest possible level to generate new high-tech ideas. Thus a generous and free educational system is an important key factor.

It must be easy and straightforward to start companies based on new ideas and get help with what is needed to start and run them.

The market mechanism is still there but it is more like a raw force that must be wielded to a good purpose just like steam power must be channelled through machinery to yield something we need.

There is thus nothing automatic behind the creation of trealth. It is instead directly dependent on a focus on trealth – not money – and politicians with great visions.

The need of Visions

> *We choose to go to the moon in this decade and do the other things, not because they are easy, but because they are hard, because that goal will serve to organize and measure the best of our energies and skills, because that challenge is one that we are willing to accept, one we are unwilling to postpone, and one which we intend to win, and the others, too.* [53]

John F. Kennedy understood the need of visions because they *"will serve to organize and measure the best of our energies and skills."* Do we understand this today?

We have a choice to make! Shall we let the economists continue to describe our reality where selfishness and greed through the invisible hand of Adam Smith is our basic religion and our confession is that money is all and can describe what we want to have? Shall we accept as desirable and advisable the idea of the economic man, homo economicus?

Or, are we instead going to accentuate the emphatic man, a human that puts empathy first and where the rational judgment is used to make decisions to help others? The goal for such a human is to increase the total sum of trealth in society and he or she understands that we can never be perfectly informed. Where work is nothing we avoid because we set up society so that work gives fulfilment, stimulates us and makes us grow and where we all get a good share of what is produced.

Do we want work that is free from harmful stress for everyone? Do we view work as an outstretched hand because we feel empathy and that makes us want to help our fellow man? Or do we view work as something to selfishly profit from?

Thus, are we going to build our visions on homo economicus or on the emphatic man? If we choose the latter we can start to break free and start building true wealth, trealth. Then we can focus on

---

[53] John F. Kennedy - September 12, 1962 speech given at Rice University in Houston, Texas.

generating new ideas for products and services that we need rather than things that are aimed at giving a maximum profit to ourselves. And doing this are we going to admit the central dominating factor new ideas – new technology – has for enabling us to accomplish this? Especially if not only a few shall enjoy the good life. That, increasing this *enabling* technology must be a first in our thinking but that it must be subject to or true needs as human beings? That fair trade, that the environment is kept free from pollution and that other *human aspects* are also central?

The time we live in now is perhaps different from the time when John F. Kennedy spoke. It is as we have been made smaller. Instead of human beings with visions, daring, an ability to experience the feelings and thoughts of others we have been reduced to money mongers. It should not have to be like that. From the same speech Kennedy held in 1962:

> "William Bradford, speaking in 1630 of the founding of the Plymouth Bay Colony, said that all great and honorable actions are accompanied with great difficulties, and both must be enterprised and overcome with answerable courage."

Thus, the challenge we face today is not new. Again we are called to do "great and honorable actions."

However, perhaps there has been major shift in what are great and honourable actions? Is it that today that just means to get rich. Preferably filthy rich? That the truth is simply that we have abandoned the basics of the Christian creed? Instead of creating things of utility we worship Mammon. Instead of concerning ourselves with the needs and problems of other human beings, as Jesus always did, we have become selfish and lovers of money.

> "He who has been stealing must steal no longer, but must work, doing something useful with his own hands, that he may have something to share with those in need." [Ephesians 4:28, NIV]

> "No servant can serve two masters. Either he will hate the one and love the other, or he will be devoted to the one and despise

the other. You cannot serve both God and Money." [Luke 16:13, NIV]

What do you think? Perhaps this is something the human race has to face up to again and again? So why do we not do that today again? What is stopping us?

> "None are more hopelessly enslaved than those who falsely believe they are free." [Johann Wolfgang von Goethe]

I do believe that one thing that do stop us are the shortcuts we use. Thus an important thing for us to constantly do is to ask ourselves, why did we arrive at this particular viewpoint? What shortcut did we use? Is this a shortcut that we want to use? If we are to become able to build a better society we must thus first see through the simplifications that lead us wrong.

Then we can build a better society together where we contribute as we can when we build a better more human world.

I do not suggest a new vision of us going to Mars even though that is a good and great vision. But I do suggest that we get visions of how to build trealth. So what about a vision to replace our gasoline eating cars with cars running on electricity? How about replacing old public communication systems with new ones built on new technology such as for instance monorails?

Add your own visions for creating true wealth, trealth!

Smaller visions perhaps than the vision of John F. Kennedy but let's together create a lot of them! And *all* of them should involve a more human based production based on fair trade.

You decide what visions you want for yourself, your friends and your kids. It is your future too!

Summary

We have a choice to make! Shall we let the economists continue to describe our reality where selfishness and greed through the invisible hand of Adam Smith is our basic religion and our confession is that money is all and can describe what we want to have? Or, are we going to go for true wealth, trealth?

Are we going to admit the central dominating factor new ideas – new technology – have for enabling us to create new true wealth? Do we understand the need of visions? And are we going to build our visions on homo economicus or on the emphatic man?

You decide what visions you want for yourself, your friends and your kids. It is your future too!

Appendix, More about Functions

The very meaning of the term "function" varies. However, the characteristic property of a function in the most abstract sense is that it relates exactly one **output** to each of its admissible **inputs**.

It is important that for each input value we get only one output value. If this is not true we run into a lot of mathematically complicated consequences which we to our infinite joy can just ignore here – if we do get one output for each input.

The standard notation for the output y of a function f with the input x is $f(\text{x})$. This is often written like this:

$$y = f(x)$$

This function defines a relation between y and x which are called variables because their values vary. The variable x is called an argument since it is an input to a function.[54]

"f" is the name of the function but we can give other names using other letters or words such as g, *mv*, *abs*, *loan* and so on. The variable y is called a dependant variable – because it depends on x. The variable x is called an independent variable.

The **domain** of a function is the set of input values for which a function is defined (that is, the values x can take). And the **range** of a function is the set of all output values that a function can produce, that is in our example, the possible values of y.

A function defines a rule between the output and the input. A simple such rule may be given like this:

$$y = 2x + 1$$

---

[54] To avoid confusion with the more general meaning with the word "argument" I mostly refer to such input arguments simply as "inputs".

However, the rule can also be given by a table or a graph or by a textual description.

Functions can also be used to express more general relations. For instance the following equation can be used to express the view that a nation's competitiveness depends on three things:

$$GC_i = f(T_i, PI_i, ME_i)$$

Where:

$GC_i = Growth\ Competitiveness$

$T_i = Technology$
$PI_i = Public\ Institutions$
$ME_i = Macroeconomic\ Environment$

This function simply states the view that a nation's growth competitiveness (GC) depends on:

- The technology (T) used..
- The state of the country's public institutions (PI). (It is argued that the quality of public institutions affects the efficiency).
- The quality of the macroeconomic environment (ME).

In this case the "rule" for finding a value for $f(T_i, PI_i, ME_i)$ is of course very complex and must be determined by analysis and discussions and no direct generally usable equation is available.

However, note, that even if we have no easily described rule we can thus use this notation to make statements. We can express our view, summarize our argumentation using this notation. For instance, we can say that something is not described as well with an equation like this:

$$y = mv(x)$$

And that we instead need an equation like the following to describe what we think is true:

$$y = mv(x, z) \ ^{55}$$

That is, y does not only depend on one input x but is much better described as depending on two inputs x and z. [56]

We can also express general behaviour of an equation by introducing the derivative:

$$y = mv(x), \qquad mv'(x) > 0$$

This expresses two things. First, that the function called mv depends on one input variable x and, secondly, that if x increases so does y and if x decreases so does y.

In this example y depends on only one input x and that is why we can write the derivate like $mv'(x)$ because there is only one possible input that can vary! However if the function depends on more than one input we need to state which input it is that we vary.

For instance, a function $f(x, t)$ depends on two inputs, x and t, so we need to indicate which input that we vary:

$$\frac{\partial f(x,t)}{\partial x} \qquad or \qquad \frac{\partial f(x,t)}{\partial t}$$

These are called partial derivatives.

---

[55] Please note, the order of arguments does not matter. Thus we could equally well have written the equation like this $y = mv(z, x)$. This mean exactly the same as our $y = mv(x, z)$.

[56] The variables x, z are thus called independent variables and y is called a dependant variable because it depends on the independent variables. This is often taken one step more in abstraction among economists, to ensure we find it difficult to understand I guess. Thus an exogenous variable is a factor whose value is independent from the states of other variables in a system/model. And an endogenous variable is a factor whose value is determined by the states of other variables in a system/model. The explanations are usually a bit more confusing including statements that the system should be causal for instance. But we do not need to know that here really so lets leave it.

The functions in this book are derived from the argumentation and the discussion that leads to one or several conclusions. If you agree with these conclusions there should not be any problems with the functions. However, if you do not agree with the conclusions the functions will be equally disagreeable to you and there is then of course nothing that demands that you accept them!

Because this book does not go much into the deeper details of setting detailed and exact formulas for the functions used it could be argued that the use of functions should be avoided and that rules should be expressed using textual descriptions instead.

The first argument for using functions is that they do give a well known and defined context for descriptions that make it easy and natural to express thoughts in a very concise manner. This avoids unnecessary text and also makes it easier to focus on the ideas and to refer to them by simply referring to the name of the function.

Another reason for using functions is that it is a natural way of expressing thoughts when we want to remain at an abstract level. It is also a common way to work when for instance programming where it is natural to start with a high level design, going to a more detailed design and finally arriving at code. In fact, if we want to describe the inner workings of a program, a high level design description is a more appropriate tool to start with than being immediately presented with the sum total of all code that constitutes the program.

The goal of this book is not to give functions that in a detailed way measure the level of technology and so on – even if that could be done! The reason for using functions is a reason of being concise when summarizing the arguments presented in this book.

And of course, because economists use the language of mathematics to impress us, we want to do the same thing ☺

Summary

Functions in this book are used to express ideas and arguments in a short, compact form. This avoids unnecessary text and also makes it easier to focus on the ideas and to refer to them.

The functions in this book are thus derived from the arguments and the discussion that leads to one or several conclusions. If you agree with these conclusions there should not be any problems with the functions.

However, if you do not agree with the conclusions the functions will be equally disagreeable to you and there is then of course nothing that demands that you accept them!

Index

true wealth 6by9 v10_7e_createspace, 2014-03-26.

www.ingramcontent.com/pod-product-compliance
Lightning Source LLC
Chambersburg PA
CBHW051713170526
45167CB00002B/647